Reflections
on San Francisco Bay

Reflections on San Francisco Bay

A Kayaker's Tall Tales
Volume II

John Boeschen

Contents

To Peggy, who loves rocks, water, and the evening light on the ridge.

Introduction

December 2001 has just stormed by . . . and I mean really stormed by. In the last 31 days, the San Francisco Bay Area has been pelted with 25" of rain, more in some places, less in others. Not since 1956 has so much water poured from the skies in the twelfth month.

While other recreators may have been driven indoors by the stormy weather—equestrians, speed walkers, lawn bowlers, golfers, and tennis players—we kayakers were in our liquid element.

Ahhh, the joys of kayaking! Wet weather, dry weather, it doesn't make any difference. And to ply the waters in San Francisco Bay is the white-water frosting on the cake. Mature old farts that we are, we admit to being spoiled by this place and this sport.

Most of the folks you'll meet in these stories are new to kayaking. Bum knees and bad backs (acquired through the aging process and spurred on by the jarring of mt. biking) led us to these human-sized boats in 1998. In those early days, we were three: Sam, Jay, and I. Over time, others joined our pod: Gristle, Wild Bill, Indiana, Danny, Albert, Now-'n-Again Ben, Zeke the Younger, Truckee Steve, SF Dave, Lucas, Rick, Ancient Bob, and Adam's Dad. Some of us make every paddle, others less so, and still others have come and gone, never to be seen again.

Though we have paddled elsewhere, the Bay is our main port and where most of these tales take place. In fact, most of our Thursday outings are in San Pablo Bay—the northern most part of San Francisco Bay—along the shores of Marin County. If you want to be real nit-picky, the vast majority of our paddles are confined to the swath of water bound in the north by Buck's Launching (close to the city of San Rafael) and in the south by Schoonmaker Cove (in the city of Sausalito and just a short float to the Golden Gate Bridge).

The tales in this book originally were reports emailed to friends after each of our Thursday paddles. The 58 short stories that appear here were written between October 2000 and November 2001. As the title of this tome (Vol. II) implies, there is an earlier volume of stories: *Reflections on San Francisco Bay: A Kayaker's Tall Tales* (no volume reference). These stories cover the period from August 1998 to September 2000.

Whichever book you happen to be thumbing through, enjoy and happy paddling.

1. Coho

Concessions are good. Several years ago after an impromptu snappage of my collar bone (preceded by earlier clavicle anomalies, disjointed fingers, rearranged arms, bruised and embarrassed ribs, and other various bends and breaks), I was notified that, henceforward, I was to heal before coming home.

I am temporarily on crutches now, having—after a 20-year hiatus—gone jogging up the south-bound lane of Highway 101 just north of Sausalito. I felt invigorated at the time, I really did; the moon was full and the lights of oncoming traffic lit up the road like an Olympic stadium. I'm sure I could have gone the distance if my calf muscles had been more willing.

But the good news is I'm home, even though I'm not totally healed. Cleaning the bathrooms for the rest of my life (at minimum, once a week) is a fair concession. I can live with it. Sort of.

The start of Thursday's paddle involved a minor concession, too. We tried to launch out of the site Gristle spotted last week along the southern Tiburon coast, but on arrival, we all conceded that the little inlet wasn't as good a low-tide put in as we had originally thought. So we drove over to Schoonmaker Cove in Sausalito, which has a fine little sandy beach suited to high- or low-tide launches.

Today was a rather special occasion: Gristle was taking his new hand-made, wood kayak on her maiden voyage. For those of you who are kayak literate, Gristle purchased a Pygmy Coho build-it-yourself kit three weeks ago and has been working none-stop on the sleek vessel ever since. We're not sure, but we suspect he may have set a world record for completion time.

After the traditional champagne toast and a bit of bubbly splashed on the boat's pointy bow, we set off to Angel Island. With the proud (but obviously sleep-deprived) Gristle leading the way, the six of us cut a rather dashing collective figure on the water. Besides Gristle and myself, Jay, his friend Mike, Indiana, and Mad Max—a paddler from Colorado—made up our spiffy little flotilla.

On our paddling card this evening was an appreciation party for last weekend's Angel Island to Tiburon swim volunteers. The party was in Sam's Bar 'n Grill right on the water and directly across from Ayala Cove on Angel Island. Time was bountiful, so we decided to paddle up Raccoon Straits and visit the cove before cruising over to the free eats and drinks.

Raccoon Straits has an attitude. It can be Walt Disney innocent and complacent, then morph, unannounced, into a roiling, green-faced Wicked Witch of the West. During the first part of our trek toward Ayala Cove, the Raccoon was all sugar plum ferries. Then, quite suddenly, a ripping green conveyor belt of 1-2.5-foot-high waves roughly 100 yards wide and running parallel to the coast surfaced. We made a dash into the heart of the belt and caught some good slash-and-dice rides.

The conveyor belt vanished as abruptly as it had appeared. One moment we're steaming along at a dandy pace in the middle of nicely formed chop, the next we're motionless in the middle of the Sargasso Sea. I think that little amusement ride may have been the Goddesses' way of helping Gristle test the seaworthiness of his Coho—which turned out to be quite seaworthy.

After another round of champagne on Ayala Cove's sandy shore, we paddled a nautical mile over to Sam's and parked our boats on the dock out back. Even though quite a crowd had gathered, we had no problem commandeering our own private table by a large picture window (it may have been the water puddling around our chairs that kept the other guests at bay).

Well, it certainly was a feast. Numerous trays of French-speaking hors d'oeuvre and bottles of Australian-accented beer found a welcome home on our salty table top. When the last stuffed mushroom and seasoned chicken wing had been devoured and we had been asked to leave by the authorities, it was 9 PM. The moon was close to full and it's doppelganger spread unbroken across Raccoon Straits.

We paddled slowly down the Straits toward Richardson Bay and Sausalito, not wanting to hurry the evening. At the

Raccoon's mouth, we paused a moment to take in the view of the Golden Gate Bridge, white lights strung along suspended cables and both towers glowing soft orange. Our view slowly spun from the bridge to the illuminated hills of San Francisco, then to streaming lights along the East Bay shore, on around to the silhouette of Mt Tam, a darker shade of charcoal than the sky behind it, and finally back to Sausalito and the Golden Gate.

We had unknowingly stopped on a slow-moving eddyline, the space where two opposing currents rub shoulders. This eddyline was spinning us in a counter-clockwise direction past the four corners of the compass and all the postcard picture-perfect landmarks in between. We sat in our boats for a long while, backtracking in time before pushing on.

That's when the serenity of the evening took a bathroom break. Not far beyond Tiburon's revolving point, Indiana rolled over in his boat. I didn't notice anything unusual about the water, he just rolled over. A few minutes later, the dark form of a catamaran loomed ahead of us.

"Let's see if you can paddle through it," Indiana challenges. I have my doubts, but before I can voice them, Gristle scoots ahead and easily glides between the catamaran's center hull and outer pontoon. Well, if he can do it . . .

But I can't. Without any room to use my paddles, I slam noisily into the boat. I push off on the metal plating directly above me and immediately capsize. Awkwardly swimming the ski out, I repeatedly bang it against the underside of the bigger boat, sounding like Ringo Starr beating out a rough rhythm to Helter Skelter.

When I exit, four people are looking down at me from the stern of the catamaran. They're laughing, not shooting rubber bullets, which is fortunate. Before I have time to apologize, Gristle, who is sitting 25 yards away, goes belly-up in calm water.

Indiana is there jaunty-on-the-spot, but calls out for more help. Gristle's boat does not yet have bulkheads and immediately fills up with water and is dangerously close to deep sixing. I climb back on the wobbly ski and start to paddle over, but one of the guys from the catamaran has jumped into a rubber zodiac and shoots past me. But before he can get to the rescue site, Mad Max coalesces out of the darkness and, together with Indiana, pulls Gristle out of the drink.

Gristle and his boat upright, pumped out, and afloat, we say our goodbyes and apologies in a lump to the catamaranites, and paddle without further incident back to Schoonmaker Cove.

It's 10:45 PM before the boats are loaded and we roll onto the freeway, heading for home. Just beyond the Sausalito overpass, my paddle struggles loose from its moorings in the back of the pickup and, in a suicidal pique, hurls itself onto the hard, unforgiving freeway. A quarter mile up the road, I pull over and jog back to collect the mangled shards.

You know the rest (btw, if anyone has information on self-cleaning bathrooms, please email me ASAP).

Stats

Distance: 7-8 miles.
Speed: Impressive with conveyor belt assist.
Time: Pretty late.
Spray factor: Substantial with champagne assist.
Dessert: Early afternoon giant chocolate chip cookie at Maggie's; late night chocolate milkshake sugar fix at In-and-Out Burger.

2. Sailor's Delight

Red sky in the morning,
Sailors' warning.
Red sky at night,
Sailors' delight.

Maybe not blood red, but the sky definitely took on an intense yellow-orange glow as the sun slipped behind Pilot's Knob. "Delight-" full was almost what the evening turned out to be.

For those nurtured on adrenaline, the paddle offered few bone-rattling, hair-parting thrills. Watching Indiana capsize three times in as many inches of water before he could even push away from the launch ramp was as close as we got to a tingle all night.

Aside from Indiana's antics, the launch was a good one. We (Gristle, Jay, Indiana, and I) showed up at Bruno's concrete ramp just as the day chimed 4:30 PM. The harbor's new policy is to charge kayakers a $5 launch fee, but the harbormaster had just locked up the till and told us to have—and I quote—a "delightful evening."

On that good omen, we paddled around the east corner of the breakwater and headed to the beached home of the fellow who sold us the surf ski several months back. Generally, if you show up somewhere uninvited and hang around long enough, I've discovered most folks will toss cookies and juice your way just to get you moving on. If it doesn't happen within five minutes, forget it.

Fortune colors an ocher evening sky, and the ski's former owner was home. We put out, shook hands all around, and talked kayaks on the little strip of sand. He was much impressed with the rudder Gristle and I had affixed to the new stern, but apparently not impressed enough to offer us cookies and juice.

With growling stomachs and sandpapered throats, we shoved off for the hopefully more receptive spinsters, Grindle and Myrtle. Often stone-faced agents of weird water, the sisters were behaving like genteel tea party hostesses this evening. "Please pass the mint cookies. More Earl Gray? My, what a lovely doily." It was really uncharacteristic of the old gals, but I suppose we shouldn't have expected anything different with them entertaining slack waters. Ignored, we cast off once again with nothing tasty to show for our impromptu visit.

On the leeward side of 50, I find Grindle and Myrtle intriguingly honest, especially for not camouflaging their age, even when they act like prissy old high-society dames. No hair tinting for these women—their domes are just as white as the day seagulls first took to calling them home. And nowhere will you find skin as rough and craggy as theirs. When you go face to face with the sisters, you know who you're dealing with.

Not so the bay, who couldn't settle on a single face for its evening's performance. At times silky smooth, the surface would catch our reflections with photorealistic perfection. Then funhouse-mirror spectres would grab center stage, oddly magnified by watery cellulite lumping up just under the surface like ticking in a bed; peaked rolls here and rounded depressions there popeyed reflections into comic-strip distortions. Cycling through more faces than Eve, the water would flow full circle and liposuction itself back into mirror perfection, hiding one set of faces for another.

At Chard Island, the overhead lights went dim, and the bay's theater was drowned out by darkness. With the time change glooming at month's end, artificial illumination has become a subject of increased paddling interest. In the small world of kayaks, being seen pulls rank over seeing. This last week, a discussion about proper lighting for kayaks raged through the Bay Area Sea Kayaker's (BASK's) listserv—literally devolving into digital fisticuffs. But when the final virtual blow was struck, most BASKers agreed to agree on a basic set of rules: a white light towards the rear of the boat and a red-green combo towards the front.

One member suggested two additional colored lights: one glowing when paddlers are pumped up on adrenaline and another when they're mellowed out on endorphins. Approaching vessels could set their course according to a kayaker's color-coded, hormonally-induced physical and emotional states: stay clear of adrenaline-charged paddlers / share sunsets with those mellowed out on naturally-occurring endorphins.

For our Thursday night paddles, a third color would be handy, one for a little-studied hormone that routinely permeates our group's endocrine systems: lollygagephrine.

Rounding Chard Island, great doses of this slow-paced hormone had commandeered our bloodstreams, and we muggled back to Bruno's hoping another boater might take notice, sympathize with our out-of-whack chemical imbalance, and offer cookies and juice (one of few known antidotes to high lollygagephrine levels). But it wasn't to be.

One last chance to zonk the hormone briefly floated our way in the guise of freshly baked cookies, their thick, warm aroma wafting over from Bobby's Fo'c's'le. But by the time my ski and truck were securely shackled together, only 10 minutes separated me from a promised appearance at the local high school's Fall music festival (during which my youngest son was to solo on the electric bass at an unannounced time).

The bad news was I didn't have time to eat before the performance. The good news was the school always serves cookies and juice at show's end.

Stats

Distance: Six miles.
Speed: Nothing above a lollygag.
Time: Two point five hours.
Spray factor: None.
Dessert: My son soloed at the very end of the concert, three very full hours after the show started. Unfortunately, the school didn't have their traditional cookies and juice for us loyal-to-the-end parents, and my levels of lollygagephrine popped to a record high. Recovery has been sluggish, and I've had to up my cookie intake to drag the hormone down to normal levels.

3. Tule Boats

Indiana made it around the mosh pit, but when I shouted to him, he looked to his left and saw the bay drop away with stomach-souring speed to a rocky bottom. Soaking that in, he wisely decided to turn around and head back, which was a good idea because it set him up to salvage some of the gear floating near Gristle's capsized boat by the breakwater.

At the time, I was novicing my ski through the hyperactive dance floor by the corner of Horseshoe Cove's big, boulder-strewn breakwater. I didn't see the bay drop away from Indiana, and I didn't see Gristle roll over in the rocks that were holding the water back from the harbor. I was too busy—and a little too spooked and jacked up on adrenaline—to turn my head anywhere beyond straight ahead.

We had launched out of Horseshoe Cove—just a couple easy strokes north of the Golden Gate Bridge—into a windless, calm harbor. Twenty-five yards beyond the harbor's mouth, however, a conveyor belt of ripping water churned towards the Gate. Though relative landlubbers when it comes to intuiting the up-and-down emotional swings of the bay, we had, prior to launch, consulted our tide charts and guessed this kind of aggressive behavior might confront us.

We also figured we'd be able to paddle north towards Sausalito against a slightly slower current if we hugged the shoreline, then yo-yo back to Horseshoe and catch a free ride with the last of the quick ebbing current. Might have worked, only we didn't factor in the weird behavior of the water close to the lumpy breakwater.

Heading north around the harbor entrance, we saw the jumbled commotion up ahead, but reckoned to bypass it by following a less treacherous watery singletrack that just then was weaving between the funny water next to the breakwater and the blitzkrieging conveyor belt further out. We succeeded for about 100 yards, until we bounced by that frenzied north corner, where a mosh pit of activity was revving up.

Indiana pulled off some pretty fancy moves, managed to hang on to the singletrack, and got beyond the frenetic dancers. Gristle, meanwhile, moved away from the uppity crowd toward the rocks lining the pit. Trying to dance his way between the stoned boulders and a fisherman's nearly invisible dangling line, he was tripped up by a rogue wave and rolled over.

I remained trapped in the mosh pit, the adolescent water hopping up and down to a chest-thumping sound track of multiple Yoko Ono's. I was paddling pretty hard, every stroke a brace to keep me upright, but making no forward progress against the heady dancers. Every few strokes, discordant frets of water from the crowded pit would gush up and pummel me, first one way, then another.

Eventually, the bobbing heads tired of the geriatric intrusion, spun my boat around their crested domes, and handed us over to the stoned faces along the breakwater, who, by that time, had worn themselves down to a frazzle and were just hanging out along the wall. Indiana roamed undisturbed among this tired, sweating enclave and salvaged most of the flotsam from Gristle's kayak. Once I rescued my own breath, I managed to pull the old guy's trade-mark $40 hat from the rough clutches of a punk rock. While Indiana and I did our duty at sea, Gristle lugged his boat up on top of the breakwater and ensconced himself on steady land while he waited for rescue.

Maybe wiser for our experiences, Indiana and I paddled back to the harbor, drove out to retrieve Gristle and his boat, loaded the remaining kayaks on our cars, and headed to Schoonmaker Cove and Richardson Bay for a much more civilized evening paddle in waters slow-dancing to the gentle tunes of Harry Belafonte and Bing Crosby.

Thursday's paddle contrasted sharply with Tuesday's, mainly because we didn't kayak Tuesday. We did, however, watch a group of kids paddle out of Heart's Desire Beach on Tomales Bay in the warm clutches of perhaps the last Indian Summer day of the year. A friend of Gristle, Charlie K., had helped a group of local 9-

and 10-year-old school kids build traditional tule reed boats as part of their schools' curricula. The boats, based on Coast Miwok, Ohlone, and Titicaca Indian designs, vaguely resembled kayaks in their long, narrow-beamed elegance.

The youngsters built two boats, an 18-footer and and a 12-footer. Charlie built his own sleek, single-person 8-footer. The bigger boats could carry up to four crew members, and each boat was made from bundles of carefully packed tule reed tied together with hand-woven cords of cattail fiber. Gristle's eyes grew big when he learned the kids had assembled their craft—once all the materials had been gathered—in a week's time (he was just then putting the finishing touches on his own hand-crafted wood kayak and had spent three weeks in the doing).

The big test—float or sink—came with the boats' maiden voyage that morning. To the kids' delight—and the adults' relief—the prehistoric vessels were quite seaworthy and proudly plied the coast along Heart's Desire numerous times without serious nautical incident. Unlike other paddlers, whom I won't mention by first or last name, the kids and their boats remained dry and right-side-up, mosh pits and Eskimo Rolls the furthest thing from their minds.

Stats

Distance: Depends on which way you're going, where you are, and who you're with.
Speed: Ditto.
Time: Just flies by.
Spray factor: Yes, indeed, if you're foolish enough to be near a breakwater during a ripping tide.
Dessert: Sweet Irish Kisses at Joe's.

4. Seattle

The shadow's edges sharpened on the tunnel wall the closer I paddled. The congealing figure's cadence even matched my own: when my right blade broke the water's dark surface, his left would disappear into a fuzzy gray area at the bottom of the wall.

With only a faint glow from the shadow's screen illuminating the long narrow space, drifting off course and scraping the boat's bow alongside either of the two narrowly spaced walls was inevitable. When this happened, holding my paddle submerged in the water to stern-rudder helped angle the boat back toward the stream's middle. During one of these recoveries, I glanced up and noticed the shadow kayaker hadn't stern ruddered . . . his paddle continued to circle while my own rested in the water.

One possible explanation for this contrary behavior: my darker, shadowy side was making the big split, navigating it's own course, as it were. The other possibility was that the sun was setting behind the far exit that lay just the other side of the curve I was approaching, and the last of the afternoon's light was projecting Indiana-(who had paddled ahead)'s shadow onto the facing wall.

This scientific explanation is perhaps the most logical, but it's also rather hum-drum. (Fortunately, we live in a world where you can choose your own reality, just as most of us will do tomorrow at the voting booth. Will it be a slightly off-kilter reality or a continuation of hum-drum, I wonder?).

The tunnel under Highway 101 is as far as the yo-yo goes. After catching up with Indiana at tunnel's end and spinning the boats 180 degrees around to face back toward Buck's, he and I paddled back out with Gristle to reconnoiter with Sam, who'd gone to port before the subterranean light show to watch a local middle school cross-country race that paralleled the creek.

On our float back to Buck's, Indiana spied a catamaran bobbing lightly at anchor. Ignoring my warning that the boat's split hull was too low to paddle under, he headed in. He did great until the far end. There, the scene degraded into a typical B-grade movie for our group: overturned boat with two arms flailing aimlessly toward the surface. Only this time there was a difference; one long, skinny arm reached up through the hazy depths and somehow managed to snag a grasp on a purse-sized net hanging from the bow of the catamaran. With a mighty jerk, Indiana righted himself and the kayak in one single, fluent motion . . . without having fallen out.

It was our group's first Eskimo Roll (net assisted or otherwise)! We had finally entered the world of BIG-TIME kayaking.

Dripping with pride and a smear or two of bottom goo, Indiana led our dandy little group back to Buck's. We neared the docks around 5 PM, just as the shadowy side of daylight was descending. Still pumped by Indiana's Roll, Gristle, Indiana, and I paddled out into the bay as far as the first duckblind before side-stroking through shallow, ebbing water back to Buck's, then on to Joe's, and eventually home.

The next morning, Jay picked me up at 5 AM for an early flight to Seattle. Just before the twelfth stroke of noon, we were test-paddling Mariner-brand kayaks in Seattle's Lake Union. Since his recent nuptials to Eileen, a speedy female sculler, Jay has been desperately seeking a fast, seaworthy kayak. After several hours of tooling around the lake in as many different vessels in gorgeous weather, the newlywed chose the boat of his whetted dreams, made a deposit, and immediately began to flounder in a rip tide of consumer's remorse.

To dampen his anxiety, Jay, his Seattle buddy Tom, and I headed up to Anacortes 75 miles north of Seattle for an overnight paddle. The evening before, Seattle was deluged with heavy wind and rain. That morning, however, was picture postcard perfect, though the postcard frayed around the edges on our northward journey. By the time we reached the Eddyline kayak outlet store in Anacortes—source of our rented kayaks and jumping off spot for the San Juan Islands—we had caught up with the tail end of the storm that had dumped on us in Seattle the previous evening.

"The small craft warning advisory is almost up," the guy behind the counter announced, "but since it's not, which of our boats do you want to rent?"

Before the advisory could be upgraded to disappointing, the three of us were paddling through choppy waters under chunky gray skies. A couple hours into our marginally uneventful journey, Saddle Bag Island loomed large on our beclouded horizon. The windward side dared us to land—went so far as to double-dog dare us—but we showed uncharacteristically good sense and paddled around to the gentrified waters on the island's lee to beach our craft.

We scuddled right out of the baby-butt-smooth water onto the narrow beach on a runway of slick, green seaweed. Wary of the weight we'd been lugging behind our bulkheads, we located the heaviest offender and downed it right there on the beach along with a slab of cheese, a spread of humus, and a baker's dozen of small pita bread.

The volume of our gear under control, we hiked the remaining stuff up a stubby cliff to an excellent little site, set up camp, and launched the boats back into remarkably calm seas. Dot Island was a flat-bottomed stone's skip away, and we headed in that direction. Earlier, Tom claimed to have spotted a bald eagle perched high a top a tree overlooking the north side of Dot. Indeed, the noble bird was there, majestically guarding its domain.

The three of us became the big bird's center of attention. Slowly drifting past, I could feel the weight of her eyes against my vulnerable back. Just as I reached a space where it became awkward to twist around in the cockpit for a last glimpse, another eagle, the underside of it's outstretched wings catching the day's afterglow, soared into view high overhead. This one slowly circled down into a nearby tree with controlled effortlessness. Spectacularly clean and simple.

One set of piercing eyes following us was disconcerting; two sets was down right unnerving. Not wishing to become part of the couple's carrion for a future flight, we paddled on. On our round-about course of nearby island splashing, we encountered habor seals, gulls, cormorants, herons, and a cast of other celebrity creatures I'm not on a first-name basis with. Of all the birds and beasts, the eagles, though intimidating, get top billing on my marquee.

Back at camp by first dark, we built a fire, cooked a hearty meal, talked for a spell, and were nestled fast asleep in the warmth of our dry sleeping bags by 6 PM.

The wind picked up sometime before midnight and howled a fretful tune. Piqued by the Siren's cries, the waters whipped themselves into a staccato fury and pummeled our little beach without let up into the early morning hours. Though Tom said it was ok and I shouldn't worry, I could feel the waves' white-nailed fingers percussing on our boats, which we had left untethered on the spindly beach.

In the cold predawn hours, the two eagles from the hood added their throaty calls to the stormy concert. With 12 hours sleep under my fleeced pants, I couldn't take the suspense any longer. I crawled out of the tent, bumbled over to the edge of the cliff 10 yards away, and looked down. The boats were still there, behind a big drift of wood, right where we had left them the night before. Pushed maybe just a smidgen toward the cliff.

During oatmeal with brown sugar and blended-in banana, the wind eased into a cool pianissimo. By the time camp was broken and the pieces carefully packed in kayaks, the sea, instead of scripting a peaceful duet, scored itself into a cold, choppy (and somewhat confused) tempo. Despite this elemental discord, we crossed without incident back to Anacortes and 25-cent showers.

Twenty-five cent HOT showers. It was very good.

Stats

Distance: Far out.
Speed: Five hundred by air, three by sea.
Time: Splendid.
Spray factor: Considerable.
Dessert: Oh yes.

5. Washington

Wispy tendrils of ghostly fog drifted across the circles of light high above our frosty heads. I could imagine General George Washington paddling through the chunky ice flows on the Schuylkill River on his way to Valley Forge back in the winter of 1777-78, stopping only briefly to skip a Sacagawea dollar coin clean across the river's sluggish expanse, slicing in half a cherry tree on the far bank.

Though historically accurate in a fashionably revisionist way, this description of Washington only partly paralleled my own situation Thursday eve. Far from Valley Forge, I was sitting inside my son's high school auditorium with my lovely bride listening to the school's chamber music program. The temperature outside the old building was in the low 50s - high 40s; inside it was cold enough to shatter the metal bayonets on the ends of the red coats' long-barreled muskets.

Mr. Peabody, the school's celebrated maestro, apologized for the arctic conditions inside the cavernous room, explaining that there wasn't enough money in the district to rehabilitate the aged furnace. And even if the old gas-fired behemoth was in working order, the odds were agin' the beast's heated breath warming our shivering bodies. . . the music department's funds having been slashed to the marrow prior to school's start.

Where's this booming economy I've been hearing about? Marin County is supposedly one of the richest, and the high school can't fire up the heat for a cool music performance. Can't even ante up the dinero to buy stands to hold the music. Even my favorite eatery, Gourmet Taco, has gone the way of the old, lifeless furnace: the three-table cafe couldn't afford the new lease on the Taco Bell shell they were inhabiting and have sadly vanished into the boom's wasteland.

If we're lucky, maybe the ghost of good ol' George'll toss some of them gold-colored coins our way.

But enough of my mewing and complaining. The concert was great, my youngest son wowed the crowd of ice cubes with his solo on the bass guitar, and I managed to tumble into a warm bed before the clock struck 22:00.

Part of my cold outlook probably is attributable to exiting the brittle surf ski onto a frozen mud beach 45 minutes before the music commenced. I don't think I ever defrosted from the paddle, even though I was farsighted enough to pack an extra thick sweater in my bag of traveling gear. Not to mention wool socks and high-topped boots.

The subsonic economic boom aside, an event I have been able to cash in on the last month has been celestial. One morning a week I pedal with a friend along our saw-tooth ridge. Of late, we've been starting out in utter darkness, the stars and sundry planets twinkling in the domed dark overhead. By ride's end, we've witnessed the sunrise and returned home fully enlightened. On Thursday's paddle, Gristle, Jay, Sam, and I immersed ourselves in the negative of this picture, starting out with a full contingent of lumens and ending in the deep global shadow that succeeds dusk.

The 3 PM launch was accompanied by a tatter of wind and jostling seas. We cruised the backside of Chard Island, the harvest season not too far distant, but could only spot Australian lettuce tufting in patches along the high tide line. Seeking only dark greens and a bit skeptical of landing on the rock strewn beach at low tide, we paddled on in the general direction of the Two Sisters. But a combination of feisty wind, white-capped waves, and a general malaise steered us back towards our point of origin.

Sam, festering to finish an irksome job due the next day for a cash-paying client, bailed and finessed his way through the bunched waters back to his car. The rest of us bid him adieu and continued in our directionless ways. Within a few clicks of a stained-glass-window sunset, Jay announced that he, too, had to abandon ship, and he headed back. Indifference at the helm, Gristle and I agreed to accompany him to Bruno's.

At a spigot of rock sticking out from the mainland a half mile from the harbor's entrance, Jay abruptly ran his Tupperware Dolphin between two ragged rocks, wedging himself securely in place. It was from this well anchored position that he explained to us something many in our generation have suspected but never been able to confirm: that our parents lied to us about Robitussin, that imperially colored cough syrup dispensed from tall, square bottles that they nipped at most evenings and that, when we youngsters asked for a sip, paternalized us with "this is for grown-ups only."

Jay deftly pulled out a bottle of the famed liquid from the dry bag he carries on the stern of his boat and, unlike our parents, passed it around freely. The liquid smelled like Robitussin, it looked like Robitussin, and it tasted like Robitussin (I admit to having climbed onto the kitchen counter as a youth and rummaged around in the cupboard above the refrigerator until I found the distinctive bottle, from which I took only enough to realize that it really didn't sit well on a young palette). By all accounts, Jay's sample WAS the fabled Robitussin of our youth.

I understand now why the adults of my childhood swore by it, some, I remember, even slurring by it. And I used to think Uncle Dick a little strange for pouring it over ice, but I see the wonder of his ways now. Growing older is, indeed, accompanied by a certain degree of enlightenment.

Our throats as velvety smooth as $53 Hawaiian silk shirts, we unwedged Jay from his crevice and meandered over to the harbor entrance. Six-o'clock school functions beckoning, Jay-the-family-man continued on to dry dock and home. Gristle and I, having less urgent deadlines, shuffled on past the harbor's restless mouth and sallied down San Rafael Creek til we ran out of water just before Highway 101.

With daylight's shadow side firmly entrenched, we hightailed it back to Bruno's in record time. Though quite cold, we felt impervious to the wicked weather's weirdness. Like our parents used to say, just a little dab'll do you.

Stats

Distance: 7-8 miles.
Speed: Never really mattered.
Time: 3.5 hours.
Spray factor: Frothy.
Dessert: Vanilla wafer leftovers.

6. Hypothermia

Finally succumbing to lips trembling blue, she nervously tugged on her oversized zipper and undid a small fetish of metal teeth at the top of her Farmer Johns.

"Aha!" I thought.

"Ahem," she snarfled. "I bet we could get his body temperature up if you loaned him your Farmer Johns. You're about his size, and he really needs to conserve heat." She worried the silver zipper back to the top of her black neoprene suit, closing the tiny teeth and shutting out the possibility for further comment or suggestion.

She was right, too. The 20-something-year-old male swimmer whimpering on the cold, damp rock next to her was about my size, only leaner and more compact. His lean mass wasn't much help, though: the 54-degree Fahrenheit bay had doused his internal fires, and the frigid early morning air was sealing the whole package in a body bag of cold. His lips were six fathoms of blue.

I tossed my paddle onto the rocks and fumbled out of the kayak. First my surfing booties came off, then the thick wool socks underneath. Free of the bootie bottleneck, I struggled out of the faded blue wet suit and, with the help of the female swimmer who had pulled the mind-numbed fellow ashore, herded him into the heat-trapping neoprene. Once his feet were covered in wool and synthetic rubber, he warmed up enough to begin hobbling the last 600 yards along the rocky shore—with his swimming mate as a cushy crutch—to the start/finish line.

They had inched less than a dozen yards over the fissured boulders when a second swimmer floundered onto the rocks. Another male. Lean and well muscled, he warfled explosively on the rock, his single exhalation like the rumble of a spent bull elephant seal. Though he's wearing Farmer Johns, he's shaking violently.

A pair of gloves is stashed in the small hold of my boat. I toss them to him. About this time, the organizer of the China-Camp-Beach-to-McNear's-Beach-and-back swim paddles up in his kayak and sheds his wind-proof jacket for the morning's second hypothermic inductee. But there's no covering for the frozen swimmer's feet, and he's unable to walk across the rough rocks toward the finish.

While the meet's organizer and I are consoling the second swimmer, the first has reached a stretch of sandy beach just before the finish. We paddle over, retrieve the booties (he keeps the wool socks), paddle back to the second swimmer, he slips into the well traveled foot coverings and is able to walk out under his own power (cold fusion?).

Young, lean, well muscled guys don't do so well in this Saturday, two-mile, open water, cold swim. Older, better padded fellows seem to suffer less. Women appear to fare best of all. Me, I was doing OK in the kayak (not being lean or well muscled has a certain advantage for kayakers, too) until I parted company with my protective coverings. Stripped down to the bare essentials—my skimpy bathing suit—and sitting in the pool of bay water that always accumulates around the Dolphin's seat was . . . how can I put it . . . beyond invigorating.

Invigoration aside, escorting these open-water swimmers was a doubleheader of personal enlightenment: (1) kayakers, comparatively speaking, are a pretty intelligent lot and (2) it's best to keep your clothes on if you plan to paddle in cold water.

Adhering like Marine Glue to #2 above, I dressed like the poster paddler in a Patagonia catalog on Thursday's return to the bay: neoprene wet suit, thick wool socks, synthetic rubber booties, Gore-Tex all-weather jacket, knit cap, well insulated life vest, and two pair of gloves. My paddling buddies—Jay, Sam, Indiana, and Gristle—did the same.

Thursday's launch site was a surprise: a beautiful sandy stretch of beach within spitting distance of the guarded entrance to San Quentin State Prison. I'd've thought you'd need some sort of special status to use the beach (perhaps a listing on the FBI's 10 Most Wanted), but not so. Apparently, any petty thief is welcome.

From the prison, we paddled under the Richmond-San Rafael Bridge, past the south side of Chard Island, and over to

Myrtle and Grindle, the Two Sisters just off McNears Quarry. We got there just around slack, and the two spinsters were napping. We bangled and splashed our paddles, but to no avail. The old gals were really sawing it off and wouldn't come out to play. Not a ruffle in the water, not even a kerf. I even tried waking them with a loud orange kayaker's whistle I bought in Seattle—the salesperson said the sound it emitted could boil eggs, and though it did fry my eardrums, the ladies slept on.

The return trip to San Quentin was quite speedy, which I attributed to masterful paddling, but Gristle claimed it was more likely due to a 5-knot ebb tide running up our exhausts. A skelter of birds—terns, grebes, gulls, and what nots—also were biding their time on the ebb. During daylight hours, birds generally take to flight whenever they get wind of us. At night, though, they don't seem half as concerned, and we often paddle close to their outer fringes.

We paddled close to a score of birds Thursday night. Once though, in the just discernible distance, a tsunami of terns sensed us and took to the air, rising from the water in a black cloud that stretched across the horizon. Daylight's end was their backdrop, and, for the briefest of moments, a vertically ascending waterfall of stars followed them up. Then, just like that, the last tern and the last star were gone.

Poof.

Stats

Distance: Eight miles.
Speed: 2-6 knots.
Time: 2.5 hours.
Spray factor: 0.
Dessert: Vanilla ice cream with chocolate sauce.

7. Pumpkin Pie Meltdown

This last Thursday being Thanksgiving, the entire day was set aside for mountain biking and ritual eating. In particular, the early morning hours were reserved for the traditional Early Bird Course of the legendary Appetite Seminar over Pine Mountain. The regular start time for the Seminar clicks in at 8:00 AM; the Early Bird Course is served up at 5:30 AM.

While the Seminar has been waning in numbers (only 900 showed up this holiday compared to 1200 several years ago), Early Bird participation has caught a thermal: last year there were only two of us, this year we soared to three (me, Sam, and Accordion Tom).

The temperature was cold, the air stuffed with fog, and the fireroads slippery and laden with tire-suck. While she was up (and after we had cleared the fog's raised roofline), a Cheshire-Cat moon beamed thin wisps of light on us till we reached Smoker's Knoll (the ride's high point), where a fresh sun sketched pastels in the east for our entertainment.

We showed great restraint at Smoker's Knoll. Really, we did. The trailhead to a well known illegal singletrack (valued on the stock exchange at four nickels) was within easy poaching range, but we held back and set tire to legit fireroads only. We later learned that Pine Mountain's munificent feudal lords had dropped trees every fifty feet across the narrow singletrack to save the surrounding forest from wanton wandering.

The Appetite Seminar up and over Pine Mountain was conceived in a frenzy of sociality. Pedaling masses flock to the event to nudge shoulders and knock knees with friends, old and new. Which is why we cooked up the Early Bird Course in the first place. As we're finishing the ride down the mountain, the main group is puffing up.

"Hi, Marty."

Tchooooo. Tchoooo.

"Hey, Nick, Chris."

Tchoooo.

"Jake!"

Tchooooo. Tchooo. Tchooo.

"Walt."

Tchooooo. Tchooo.

Steaming down that serpentine hill, we scoot past just about everybody we know. Tchoooooo. Tchooo.

Though four miles remain before I face home and hearth, our ride is officially over at the Coffee Rotisserie in Fairfax. Typically, we linger over large ceramic mugs of hot chocolate and mild-mannered pastries before heading home. This year, the sexy glint of dark, roasted orange snags my eye. In the glass-fronted display case—where the Rotisserie's best kept treats promenade—are two sweet slices of pumpkin pie.

Sam and I each order a slice . . . topped with a fog of whipped cream. My slice of pie is an exquisite, melt-in-your-mouth, the stuff-dreams-are-made-of delectable. I ponder it all the way home . . . past the field behind Sunny Hills School, through the cemetery, past the old vine-enshrined mausoleum (spooky place at night), up the wooded divide, and into my garbled garage.

P-u-m-p-k-i-n pie.

Besides whetting appetites and renewing old friendships, the Early Bird Course gets me home in time to help with the day's festivities.

"Oh, you're home early."

"Yup. What can I do? How can I help?"

"Keep out of our way."

So I sit and restlessly watch Sandy and my #2 (birth order) son, Trent, prepare The Meal. Sandy's doing the Bird, smashing potatoes, candying yams, that kind of ritual stuff. Trent is scratching up pies. Pumpkin pies. He works carefully and verrrrry slowly. The pies (there are three when he finally puts the ladle down) are The Meal's piece de resistance.

My recollection of the next series of events is somewhat . . . wavery. Like looking back across a desert. I retire to my big stuffed blue chair soon after The Meal. I've committed myself to respectability, having ingested just two civilized portions of pie (a dab of whipped cream atop each). Quickly succumbing to a tule fog of contentment, I doze off.

From a dreamless sleep, I awake into a dusky throg, my mouth sweetly dry. Lurching to my feet and ignoring my surroundings, I stumble bleary eyed to the kitchen counter. Where there were three, now only one pie tin greets me. A modest greeting at that, with only a ragged nut-brown slice barely the thickness of my thumb scowling up at me. Though I discover I'm not really terribly hungry, I gobble down the measly portion before the scowl triumphs into a sneer, then scan the kitchen for the other pie tins.

They lie empty, desolate under a slow, monotonous drip in the kitchen sink.

"Why didn't you save me some pumpkin pie?" I accuse Sandy and Trent after tracking them to the living room.

Silence.

"Well?"

Louder silence.

"Hey, I only had two slices for dinner."

"Hrmmph," Sandy gronkles.

"Yeah, well look at your chair," Trent gestures.

My big blue stuffed chair is the center piece for a pumpkin pie meltdown. Dabbles of crust and shards of dark orange pudding paint a disturbing Matisse of gluttonous guilt.

I know now it was a tasteless act, for a sleep-eaten pie can have no redeeming flavor.

Stats:

Miles: 17.
Speed: 6 mph.
Time: 3.5 hours.
Spray factor: Canned.
Dessert: Just.

8. Tralfamadore

I'll buy you a plastic suit
I'll even buy you some cardboard fruit. (*Easy Rider*,
James Gurley, Big Brother and the Holding Company,
1966)

These words were tap dancing through my noggin—I don't
know why, except maybe I'd dialed into an alternate
frequency—while paddling to catch up with Jay, Indiana, and
Gristle.

We'd just lugged our boats over and around metal locks
carefully sculpted to contain the tame waters of Bel Marin Keys
while cleverly keeping riff-raff like us out. Locks, however, are not
functioning properly unless they can be opened, and our sojourn in
the civilized corpus de agua had been pleasantly uneventful. Other
than a solitary sculler, we'd had the horseshoe-shaped lagoon all to
ourselves. The only homeowner we spied was hidden behind floor-
to-ceiling pleaded green curtains watching us circumvent the locks
on our way in and, later, on our way out.

We had crossed into the Keys' inner sanctum in bright
daylight and were now withdrawing into the bay under a dark quilt
of cosmic vapors. It was the kind of clear, crisp evening that gets
your bodily juices flowing. So, while my kayaking buddies flowed
homeward on the ebb, I hung back to let my own salty waters flow.

This is not a simple proposition, particularly if the wetsuit
you're inhabiting lacks the appropriate outlets. With my own fluids
close to flooding and no handy port in sight, the first layer of
winterized clothing sacrificed is the PFD (personal flotation device)
followed closely by the all-weather Gore-Tex jacket underneath.
Once the jacket's off, the Velcro shoulder straps on the wetsuit are
within easy ripping reach. Unleashed, the rip roars into a tug that

peels the tight-fitting suit down to mid-thigh, freeing the necessary plumbing that empties the tank.

After arduously reassembling the multi-layered outfit—maybe one of Big Brother's plastic suits would be better—I give chase to my more or less bladder-challenged friends. They're too far ahead to have any substance, and I paddle alone through a swirling quilt of reflected stars that wraps itself completely around the surf ski.

It takes forever to catch the three amigos. Jay's leading the little flotilla in his Dolphin, a seaworthy Tupperware sit-on-top noted for it's versatility but not particularly for it's speed. The rest of us are in much quicker boats. Jay is clearly in work-out mode; while we relax in our sleeker craft, he's sweating up an anticipatory storm for the arrival of his own speedy vessel from the legendary Kevlar foundries of Mariner Kayaks in distant Seattle. When the phantom boat arrives, I expect we'll be seeing less of Jay, except for maybe on the clearest of days.

But for tonight, at least, we paddle as a single flock into the bay. At the channel's final twist into the wider expanse of water, twin sets of East Bay lights stitch themselves into the reflected halves of our quilt. The tide is ebbing at almost 4 knots. To avoid the quickly encroaching mud flats, we follow the deep-water channel markers—dimly outlined by the quilt's thread of light—toward our put-in under the bridge at Black Point, where the Petaluma River is break-dancing into the bay.

We're moving against the tide, and the deeper water skirting the mud flats leads us on a longer, more round-about course toward the bridge. Growling out of the darkness, hunger and fatigue jump us without warning. Though we don't have any cardboard fruit, Gristle does have a silver thermos full of hot miso. We try to raft up a table in open water, but the strong current pulls us apart.

Thoughts of hot soup toying with our hollow innards, we eventually belly up to a thick channel marker, two boats on either side of the tall wood post. With one end of a leash attached to his kayak and the other to his paddle, Indiana tosses the combo around the slippery, barnacle-encrusted marker to me. Gristle hangs onto my boat while Jay sidles up to Indiana. Straining at the leash, we down the steamy treat just as fast as Gristle can pour the warm liquid into our shared plastic cup.

Bellies sated and Indiana's leash free of the grimy channel marker, the four of us paddle toward the bridge. Two strokes past the marker, our progress is greeted by a thunderous round of applause. Gristle says it's a large mishap of ducks spooked to flight; I think the sound's more reminiscent of the eternal rapture that applauded Billy Pilgrim (of "Slaughterhouse Five" fame) when he had his first close encounter with the former porn star Ms. Montana Wildhack on the distant planet of Tralfamadore (you had to be there to appreciate it).

The applause tracks us all the way to the old train crossing just this side of the bridge. There, a stretch of trestle parallel to the shoreline can be swiveled—with the aid of large diesel-fueled engines—from the structure's mid-river resting place to connect the two banks. A spotlight with the voice of a sweet Siren sings out near a rusted ladder that climbs from the water to the trestle.

"Over here, John, over here," the torch sing-songs.

The light is calling out to me with the same force that must've swept Billy off his feet to Tralfamadore. I have to climb that ladder. I really do. At the top, a set of narrow stairs leads higher up to a rickety control shack. Inside are sets of greasy gears and levers like you see in old coal-fired locomotives.

I've never seen the trestle span the river at night. When it swings into place, you certainly have to wonder who'll be on the train that creaks across.

"Go on," the light from below whispers gently into my ear. "Pull the lever. The big one, there in the middle of the shed."

It's a very seductive whisper.

Stats

Distance: 6 or 7 miles.
Speed: A little under 2 knots.
Time: About 3.5 hours.
Spray factor: Wrong planet.
Dessert: Pumpkin pie at Joe's to celebrate Indiana's palindromic b'day.

9. Hemingway

The ferry edged by us along a parallel course 25 yards to the north. We—Jay, Gristle, and me—were 2.5 miles out in the bay west of Bezerkeley, paddling back to shore next to the old derelict pier that bisects that lengthy stretch of water. The boxy passenger boat came up on us out of nowhere, and though we were paddling in the thick of twilight, she was easy enough to spot, lit up with sparkly white lights like a noble fir on Christmas morning.

It was the melodic clinking of ice against cut crystal that turned our heads. And the low hush of voices rippling over mirrored water, punctuated now and then with throaty laughs and exclamations. Sounds and lights from a different time zone. A perfect fit for the boat, which resembled vessels from the 20s and 30s I'd seen framed on the walls of the World Trade Center in San Francisco.

Sitting behind one of the windows on the main deck facing us are two people, a man and a woman. Leaning suggestively close together over the narrow wood table that separates them, their hands—encircling clear iced drinks—almost touch one another. The ferry's interior lights are bright, and it's hard to make out the couple's features. But the clean-shaven man—perhaps in his late twenties or early thirties—looks up, and it's Ernest Hemingway, or at least his dead ringer.

And the woman? Didn't really get a good look at her, but since we're paddling in the twilight zone, it had to be journalist/poet Dorothy Parker. And I bet she's interviewing Hemingway for that famous 1929 "New Yorker" piece she's about to pen, the one where she asks, "Exactly what do you mean by 'guts'?" and he smiles back with, "I mean, grace under pressure," and then leans a little closer to her, the tips of his outstretched fingers brushing lightly against her white knuckles.

That's a good quote, and she smiles back.

Actually, we were more likely watching Midland Mutual Insurance agent, Harvey Scotnick, trying to pick up on his secretary, Nadine Flivavitz, during their office's annual Holiday Party On The Bay. He was probably quoting Hemingway (hoping the bells would toll for him later in the evening).

Which helps explain why we were so far from shore in the first place: during daylight, objects in the bay can appear closer than they actually are; at night, they're really far out.

Long before the festive phantom ferry phased by us, we were bounding on the main about 1/4 mile to the north of Berkeley's 3000'-long pier. The pier is actually 3 miles long, but only the first 3000' are usable. The rest of it has gone to the seadogs, its barnacled concrete pilings sticking out of the water like the legs of an up-ended and waterlogged millipede.

Looking at the pier's denouement from less than a mile off shore earlier in the evening, I had suggested we paddle out "because the end doesn't look that far away." Hah! After turning the kayaks around at the pier's blunt conclusion many minutes and paddle strokes later, we saw how far we'd actually departed from our senses: Berkeley had become a shadowy hillside panaroma stitched together with strings of tiny yellow lights. Very tiny yellow lights.

Shallow water during low tides has spearheaded the pier's lengthy push away from the citystate of Berkeley. The first long pier—1300 feet—was built in 1874 for ferry service from Berkeley to San Francisco. But a rival ferry business out of Oakland sunk the Berkeley venture two years later.

In 1923, the Golden Gate Ferry Company concocted a new plan to re-establish direct service between Berkeley and San Francisco. The new ferry was built for people in cars and buses (there goes the waterfront). The original pier was torn down, a new three-mile-long wharf was built, and service opened in 1929 with the inaugural voyage of the ferryboat Golden Bear.

Bad timing again. On November 12, 1936, the San Francisco-Oakland Bay Bridge opened as the world's longest steel span at 43,500 feet and doomed the hapless ferryboats to drydock.

What goes out must come back (it's a maritime rule, though the local ferries could be coming back into service at a faster clip if you asked me). Adhering strictly to the letter of the law, we ebbed back to our dock of departure on the dark side of nautical twilight. Changed into dry-land civvies, we sauntered over to the Berkeley Yacht Club, site of the Bay Area Sea Kayakers (BASK) annual Holiday party and clinked together a few glasses of holiday cheer.

Though only two-thirds of our small group were BASK members, the one-third without a membership card showed true grace under pressure when questioned by the authorities. Hemingway would've toasted his gutsy behavior.

Stats

Distance: 8 miles.
Speed: 3.2 knots.
Time: 2.5 hours.
Spray factor: None.
Dessert: Unbelievable.

10. Eskimo Roll

We put in where the sun don't shine. Actually, Marin county was gunny-sacked in a water-logged layer of thick, low, gray clouds all day. We would've been served up the same dreary reception regardless of our launch point.

Though we hit the water at Schoonmaker Cove in Sausalito by 3:30 PM, the day was already semi-dark and befuddled with rain and a pervasive fog that weighed the surface calm. Having permanently mounted half a hemisphere of impressive compass on his foredeck, Gristle wisely took a directional reading before we lost sight of the shoreline (close to instantly).

During last Sunday's paddle along China Basin in San Francisco, I was able to demonstrate my own navigational skills. In fact, I even got Gristle to briefly question the mechanical accuracy of that fancy deck-mounted compass of his. Somehow, we got into a round-robin of "Which way do you think we're going now" (Gristle) and "We're going (north, east, south, west)" (me).

I sighted on well-know land scapes and marks to lend weight and credibility to my pathfinding skills: Oakland, South San Francisco, Candlestick Park, Mt. Diablo, Mt. Tamalpais, San Francisco International Airport, Sutro Tower. The day was shamelessly clear and everything fiercely visible.

We debated heatedly over the cold waters for a rift of time.

"Which way you think we're headed now?"

"East. We're going due east."

"No! We're going southwest."

"Wait a minute. There's a plane taking off from Oakland International right over there. We're going east!"

"No, no! My compass says southwest."

So it went.

Finally, frustrated with Gristle's apparent lack of directional vision, I snatched out my own smaller Cub Scout compass . . . and confirmed his every reading. Although all my reckonings had been dead wrong, at least I'd been 100% consistent in my waywardness.

Fully aware now that I'm magnetically challenged, I blindly followed Gristle's lead behind the others (Wild Bill, Jay, Sam, and Indiana) into the directionless fog Thursday afternoon. It'd be salty revenge to report that Gristle got us totally lost in the never-ending wrap of Richardson Bay and that we finally had to holler for help and that a houseboat wife in red curlers and green face paint came to our rescue in a yellow rubber raft. But it wouldn't be true (though it does offer some colorful possibilities); the old guy led us diagonally and unerringly across the bay to distant Strawberry fields and back again. Our only mishap was overshooting Schoonmaker Cove on the return by 600 yards in the dark.

Well, actually, there were several other mishaps. All of them belonged to Sam. Near the end of our adventure, the veteran paddler couldn't stay on his surf ski regardless of where the compass was pointing. North, south, east, west—didn't make any difference. For a while, the only direction he knew was straight down.

A couple of us took a class Monday night at the Richmond Plunge that Sam might have benefited from had he been there: an introduction to Eskimo rolling. For those of you blissfully unfamiliar with this technique, the idea is to roll your kayak so it's right-side up if you happen to flip over in the water. But there's a catch: you have to stay in the boat while you do it. This is a serious catch. And let me tell you, if you think it's easier to roll a boat over while you're on the outside of the kayak looking in, you'd be right. It is (unless, of course, you can Eskimo roll).

So why learn how to Eskimo roll?

Because it looks so cool. You gain big points in the open water if you can Eskimo roll. People on party boats applaud. No telling what might happen if houseboat wives (or husbands) in green face paint and red curlers spot you. The only cooler thing might be to do a Tom Cruise over your neighborhood with one of those personal jet packs I saw demonstrated at Disneyland in 1955.

For the first part of our two-hour lesson, the instructor would pull us over toward him on the right side of our boats without letting go. The not-letting-go part was real good. Then he'd instruct us to flip our right hip and knee up hard against the inside of the kayak to right the boat while he still held on. As long as he held on, it was easy rolling.

During the second hour, the instructor rolled the boat over and away from himself on the left side and then relaxed his hold. It was not easy to roll the boat now. No, indeed. In fact, it was impossible (there was one young lad in his early to mid twenties built like Johnny Weismiller in "Tarzan, Ape Man of the Jungle" who was whirling like a Dervish after 30 minutes, but I suspect black magic or some such occult tomfoolery involving mirrors).

Hanging upside down under water, I discovered that my sense of direction does not improve. Actually, it may become worse, what with the water flooding up my nose and shorting the internal circuitry. When I tried to flip my hip and knee, I panicked because I couldn't find either. I remember them both being there when I started to roll over into the water, but like the 343 reading glasses that have recently vanished before my very eyes, so went the lower half of my body. Gone. Just like that. I tried looking around under water, but couldn't find a darn thing (no hips, no knees, no reading glasses).

When I surfaced, the instructor said maybe I should concentrate more on what I was doing with my hands.

Ha!

Stats

Distance: 5 miles.
Speed: Slower than it seemed.
Time: 2.5 hours.
Spray factor: Engulfing.
Dessert: Large slice of Punjabi pecan pie.

11. Solstice

'Twas Thurseve of Solstice, when all through the bay
Not a creature was stirring, not even a bat ray;
The dry bags were hung by the coaming with care,
In hopes that Sea Goddesses soon would be there;

The kayakers were nestled all snug in their hulls,
While visions of Eskimo rolls danced in their skulls;
And Sandy in her PFD, and I in my wet suit,
Had just settled down to a long winter's snoot,

When out on the water there arose such a splatter,
I sprang up in my boat to see what was the matter.
Away to the north I glided like a shark,
Tugged on my life vest and rowed into the dark.

The moon on the crest of a new-formed wave
Cast the lustre of twilight to objects in a sea cave,
When, what to my wondering eyes should display,
But a multi-chined kayak, tailed by eight compadre,

With a little old paddler, so lively and fickle,
I knew in a moment it must be St. Gristle.
More rapid than seagulls his cruisers they came,
And he whistled, and bellowed, and hailed them by name;

"Now, Sam! now, Jack! now, Wild Bill and Danny!
On, Jay! on Ancient Bob! on Ben and Indianie!
To the top of the swell! to the top of the squall!
Now splash away! splash away! splash away all!"

As dry heaves that before the wild chop flail,
When they meet with white water, billow out like a sail,
So up to the harbor the cruisers they drew,
With kayaks full of spirit, and St. Gristle too.

And then, in a sprinkling, I heard on the glade
The thunking and clunking of each little blade.
As I drew in my hand, and was bracing around,
Down the trough St. Gristle surfed with a bound.

He was attired all in neoprene, from his head to his bootie,
And he was soaked with seaweed and smelled like fish fruity;
A bundle of bright light he had flung on his spine,
And toward our harbor he paddled a nautical line.

His eyes—how krinkled! his eyebrows how hairy!
His cheeks like a puffer fish, his nose fast as a jet ferry!
His shoulders flung him o'er the waves with a hop,
And the goatee of his chin was as wild as the chop;

A length of spruce he held tight in his fist,
And the stroke it encircled him with a spiral twist;
And his wood blade spread the surf like grape jelly,
When he twisted around with his big old belly.

He was sent by the Goddesses, a right jolly old sea elf,
And I snarfled when I saw him, in spite of myself;
The flash of his grin and the slant of his beam,
Soon proved that he captained one merry team;

He broached not a word, but sculled straight to his work,
And filled our bags aglow; then turned with a smirk,
And laying his paddle aside of his nose,
Out the harbor atop the flooding tide he rose;

A turn he carved, while to his buddies gesturing with pride,
And away they all paddled atop a rip roaring tide.
But I heard him exclaim, ere he floated out of sight,
"Happy Solstice to all, and to all more blessed daylight!"

12. Geo-Political Landmark

We—Indiana, Ben, Wild Bill, Sam, and I—launched out of Gristle's Secret Paradise Bayo and cut north across San Pablo Bay towards San Quentin Prison and the nearby Richmond-San Rafael bridge.

The bridge is a geo-political landmark for me.

Politically, the overly large pilings that hold the span skyward remind me of Bill Clinton's undercooked, jumbo-sized thighs. White and with a girth that would make any emu proud, they conjure up an image of a Wendy's chicken burger, extra large, hold the mayo.

Now, don't get me wrong—I'm not being judgmental because of any oral office shenanigans. No, it's those first-term glossy papparazzis of the prez in running shorts lumbering by a greasy, fast-food place in D.C. that float those pale pillars of pulchritude to consciousness. I'm certainly not singling him out for his politics—'cause, for the life of me, I can't fathom much difference in his machinations and the doings of other presidents whose tenures have splashed on my shore (paddling back to Truman, if you wanna believe that).

The guys on this year's ballot are a firm grip short of a functioning paddle, too. And I ashamedly admit that I did dimple one of their chads. The only consolation I have is that my vote probably wasn't counted, what with all the disqualifications and coloring outside official lines. In fact, this election was the first in years that I've actually voted for someone listed on the ballot.

When my conscience doesn't ebb on me as it did this year, I usually scribble "Xena, Princess Warrior" on the blank line that underscores the candidates. A woman who can't be compromised, Xena is. No soft money for her, no half-hearted campaign promises, either. Royalty for the rest of us.

Which channels into the "geo" part of the geo-political significance of the Richmond-San Rafael bridge. The water on the south side of the bridge is markedly different from the water on the north. South tends to be wilder, less focused, in-your-sprayskirt, and jacked up on testy swells. North is energetic but less frenetic, more focused, subtle, and slightly crazed with wind. Mars and Venus. Hercules and Xena. And the only thing within six degrees of separating them are Bill's big, white thighs.

What a world.

Heading north this afternoon had nothing to do with gender or politics. Wind waves were running north-south, and the surest way to navigate them was head on. Indiana was particularly agreeable to this approach since he was paddling my squirrelly ski for the first time. Absent the surf ski, I had commandeered the brand new sit-in kayak that Jay had pledged heart and soul to on our Seattle pilgrimage six weeks ago.

A marvelous boat (designed for easy ocean cruising and inland waterway gallivanting), it was only reasonable that I would soon covet it for myself. Jay was out of town when the sleek craft arrived, and, at his behest, I took temporary possession. After two outings in the boat, I claimed imminent domain and salvage rights, confronted Jay with my claims, and, playing justice for all it was worth much like our Supreme Court, reached a civil understanding of the nautical laws involved, flipped a coin, and have since assumed full ownership.

Life's good when you have your way.

Now that I've staked a serious claim to a fancy sit-in, my thoughts have once again churned over to Eskimo rolls. Falling off a sit-on-top and getting back on is like reading non-fiction: straight forward and to the point. Regaining composure in an up-ended sit-in, however, is more akin to reading fiction: endings are full of surprises. Of all possible endings, rolling promises the quickest, driest, and happiest outcome.

I figure the best way to learn is to mimic experts, and those in the flow claim the best rollers are native Greenlanders. Every year, the Greenland Kayaking Association hosts a competition, and major among the events is rolling. I just got wind of this year's results (the competition ended in July, but news travels slowly by kayak), and I've been eyeballing them for pointers.

So far, what I've learned has been daunting. In the rolling competition, participants are tested on 30 different rolls. Among them are the standard roll, the storm roll, the reverse sweep roll, and the armpit roll—easy stuff like that. Things heat up with the elbow roll, the crossed-arm roll, the hand roll (no paddle), the strait-jacket roll (no hands and no paddle), and the rock 'n roll (you hang onto an 8 kilogram rock—my, oh my).

The paddle de mettle is the Walrus Pull. A rope attaches to your kayak, runs under it, and into the hands of five brutes on shore. These guys—the biggest Greenlanders the Association can find—pull the kayak 15 metres through the water, tugging on the line to flip you over. Short of tossing a harpoon their way, you use your best kayaking skills to prevent capsizing.

Fuhgetaboutit.

The only event I saw that seems to make sense for me is upside-down paddling. Then again . . .

Have a peaceful, upright new year.

Stats

Distance: 8 miles.
Speed: Satisfying.
Time: For lots of interesting things.
Spray factor: A tad.
Dessert: Hot chocolate with whipped cream and a cup of clam chowder.

13. Greenland Paddle

What an opportunity! I mean, how often do you tumble into a position where you can pull off an actual Greenland kayaking maneuver? An official maneuver at that, one sanctioned by Greenland's own famed Kayaking Association.

Oh boy.

I couldn't resist, no I couldn't. The surface of San Pablo Bay looked like it had just been treated to one of those Calistoga mud baths, its skin a bit murky but silky smooth. Not a wrinkle, not a disturbing blemish in sight. That's the kind of water it was Thursday evening.

I was paddling my new, Jay's-rightfully-relinquished-lost-in-the-flip-of-a-coin Mariner II sit-in kayak. Long, low, mean—that was me on the water. A boat length in front, Sam was smartly creasing the water's surface with his surf ski. I was paddling very quietly, oh so quietly behind. Sam didn't even know I was there. That's how quiet I was.

In high school, our track coach always said to pass the guy in front big. BIG. Make the guy wish he were somewhere else when you went by. And don't let him know you're there until you're out in front. That's how serious our coach was—he really wanted us to pass BIG. Though we lost all our meets, I remembered his words Thursday evening.

I would use the element of surprise and pass Sam BIG. And I would do it using an officially sanctioned Greenland kayaking technique.

Oh boy.

This was my plan: I would sneak up really close behind Sam, ride along in his wake for a moment or two while I primed myself for the BIG move—Greenland Paddling Maneuver

#30—and pass Sam before he could figure out what had happened. He was in for a surprise.

This one's for you coach, and I white-knuckled the paddle shaft in anticipation.

Maneuver #30 is Paddling Underwater. Without a sound, I expertly rolled the kayak over and flailed the water upside-down like a top-heavy walrus chasing a school of red herring. At the point where I was sure I had passed beneath and beyond Sam's ski (about the same time my final breath bid me aloha), I flicked my hip and knee against the inside of the kayak like they tell you to do in Maneuver #1—the Eskimo roll—to right myself in front of Sam's boat.

By the time Jay, Jack, and Wild Bill fished me out of the water, Sam was no larger than a speck of bottom gunk on my glasses. Later, at Bruno's, when I explained what had transpired, he admitted that he hadn't heard a sound, that I had been as quiet as a ring-tailed water snake in a fish hatchery. Even more gratifying, he conceded total surprise at my clever stroke of genius.

With a little more work on technique. . . .

For the past month, we've been tossing around the idea of taking the Greenland paddle plunge. Those who ply the waters with the skinny sticks claim they're more sympathetic than European blades to the aches and pains of old mariners. And the Goddesses know, the Olde Grim Paddler himself has dropped anchor on a number of my tender body parts lately.

The beauty of a Greenland paddle is that you can carve it out of a single 2" x 4". One piece, no assembly required. My kind of project. So I ambled down to the nearest lumber yard and asked where I could find a straight-grained length of red cedar. The guy behind the counter pointed to the far corner of the yard, "In that warehouse there."

The entire structure, top to bottom, was filled with red cedar. I eventually found a bin full of 8' lengths. Must've been 200 or more pieces in that bin. Now, I can glance at a slew of plastic, rotomolded poles and immediately spot the one with the straightest, tightest grain. No problemo. I was clueless, however, in this sea of cedar. Awash in a maelstrom of arboreal uncertainty, to be sure.

Fortunately, a woodsman was sorting through another bin of cedar trimmings nearby. He had a look of confidence and certainty about him.

"Excuse me," and I approached him with my dilemma. I was looking for "the perfect board to carve into a Greenland paddle, but I don't know what to look for. Can you help me?"

He eyed the scattered pile of timber I had pulled out of the bin for a minute or so. Then he sauntered over to the far end of the wreckage, picked up a piece, sighted down its length, balanced it in his right hand, sighted down the other side, brought it close to his nose for a deep whiff, then put on his glasses and scrutinized the grain.

"This one," and he handed it to me.

"How can you tell?"

"It's hard to explain," he said, "but locked up in this board is the perfect Greenland paddle. You've just got to free it."

Cool. I thanked him, bought the piece, and took it home to set that paddle loose. I hacked, and I whacked, and I carved. When my efforts started to take on the persona of a hard-edged prison warden rather than Amnesty International, I scooted over to Wild Bill's and his collection of power tools. With Wild Bill's coaching, I managed to salvage parole for the imprisoned paddle.

Had I known the woodsman at the lumber yard was really Boris Karloff, then I wouldn't've been as surprised as I was when the Bride of Frankenstein lurched out of that 2" x 4".

Strikingly tall, skinny, and with more nicks and bruises than the Italian Stallion after his first brouhaha with Apollo Creed, that paddle was really scary looking. Painfully ugly.

But it sure smelled nice, particularly after I anointed it in the bay Thursday evening. Smelled like a forest primeval, it did. Odors from the Mesozoic. Fresh without a backwash of civilization: no stains, primers, plastic resins, or varnishes to hide its true face. And it took to the water like a hush of ducklings, skimming the cold surface contours without so much as an unruly peep.

You had to be there not to hear it. Just ask Sam.

Stats

Distance: 5 miles.

Speed: Calculated.
Time: 2 hours.
Spray factor: Nonexistent.
Dessert: Key lime pie all around.

14. Storm of the Century

Last week was host to the new year's swiftest ebb tide. On Tuesday, January 9, 2001, the water level in the bay dropped from a high of 7.2 feet at 10:19 AM to a low of -1.7 feet at 5:14 PM. These ups and downs sloshed into a 6-knot ebb tide. The same speedway conditions repeated themselves on Wednesday.

A 6-knot ebb is the stuff of "free rides." To cash in, simply hop into your favorite kayak, point its bow in the direction of the flow, and watch the scenery scoot by.

Last week also was host to the Storm of the Century. The frosting on the storm's cake were weighty peals of thunder, yellow streaks of lightning, and biblical quantities of rain. The main mix was wind. Mutant strains were clocked up to 45 knots while the average breeze clicked in between 15 and 30 knots.

The upstart wind was going head-to-head with the tidal flow as well, blowing most kayaks back to their launch sites. Despite the unfavorable odds, a group of 12 BASKers (Bay Area Sea Kayakers) put out of China Camp Beach Tuesday and headed for the north tower of the Golden Gate Bridge (12 miles distant). The results were very encouraging for those of us who couldn't make the trip: out of the 12 starters, 3 made it. If they'd been a mass mailing, that would've been a 25% return. Not too shabby in anyone's marketing scheme.

Buoyant from Tuesday's positive returns, we waited for Wednesday and our chance to flow in the ebb. But the windy bay had different plans. Even unseasoned as we were to the ways of the crafty water spirits, we didn't have to go any further than our living room windows to know we'd be no match for the Sea Goddesses that day.

Thursday was no different. The Goddesses were on a three-day rave, kicking up their heels in a fast break dance. My, oh my, but those women were wild. And, rubbing salt in our wounded plans, the start of the ebb had moved to later in the afternoon. It would be impossible to reach the Gate before nightfall. No free ride for us.

Our only option was to scale down—to head out of China Camp Beach with no destination in mind. "Let the raging spirits have their way with us" seemed like a good course to follow (you fall off your bike and kayak onto your head enough times, you start to think like that).

Water was whooping over the breakwater onto San Pedro Road on the way to China Camp. Hoooh boy. I'd never seen the likes of that before and moved the windshield wiper setting from slow to fast. At the beach, San Pablo Bay had rolled big logs into the middle of a flooded parking lot. Wading through the muddy water to what was left of the beach, I watched waves break brown close to where I stood.

Fortunately, I didn't have to worry long about whether I'd be able to launch through the surf (guys have so many worries)—a posted sign claimed the beach was temporarily closed and for people with a death wish to leave. Now.

At the top of the hill overlooking the beach, I met up with Sam, Albert Wang, and his brother Tom. We voted to head north along the shore to see what was to be seen. We didn't have to go far. A jutting promontory separates China Camp Beach from Bull Head Flats, and today that spit of land was graciously holding back the wild winds and water from Bull Head.

We put our boats into a glassy smooth bay while gentle swells rolling in from a Disneyland-perfect setting lapped at our hulls. Well, no . . . not really. The setting was more like Robert Louis Stevenson's "Dr. Jekyll and Mr. Hyde." The water in the little baylet was civilized, a regular Dr. Jekyll (Dr. Walt?), all right. But the water a mere 100 yards away was Mr. Hyde.

I prefer Mr. Hyde to Dr. Jekyll. Hyde's out there for all he's worth—what you see is what you get. Jekyll is far more circumspect—nice guy one moment, a pain in the aft quarters the next. If you like film noir and deep psychoses, hang with Jekyll. On the other hand, if you want to taste the Goddesses, Hyde's your man.

We hung with Hyde and the Goddesses. They were really stirring it up, too. Crazy water. No rhythm to their dance. Three- and four-foot wind waves coming up from every direction. Caps breaking white across the boats, sterns and bows alternately lifted high then dropped back down. Hard. Whoosh . . . thunk. Whoosh . . . thunk.

Out beyond Rat Island, the party was particularly wild . . . depending on which side of the coin you were hanging onto. Heading through the frothy mix into the wind was pleasantly unnerving; you had the mind-altering illusion of control. Keep the boat pointed straight ahead and don't stop paddling. Control. Addictive, it was, that control. Hard to give up. But that's what you did when turning tail to the wind.

Albert and his brother were in a 21-foot-long tandem. A good deal of the time—at the top of cresting waves—their kayak would be perched like a teeter-totter unsure of which way to lean, long sections of bow and stern shamelessly exposed to the Goddesses long fingers. Heading into the wind was straight forward enough. Ahhhh, but with a shifty tailwind, their bow would plummet quickly down the face of a wave, then lose speed relative to the wind-driven water behind them, stalling at the bottom in the trough created by the wave in front.

If the brothers were lucky, the rear wave would pick them up again and they'd have a second chance to move forward. If they weren't that fortunate, the heaving water in back would break over their stern, submerging them in a white soup. Cream of Chaos. After three or four helpings, we all decided to head back to shore (less than 200 yards away).

In the no-man's land between Jekyll and Hyde, the Goddesses had settled down a tad. There was a distinct, flowing rhythm to their dance now, and the four of us were able to surf their long, curving swells back to our launch site over Jekyll's back. So enjoyable was the spin the water spirits had taken, we doubled back and surfed in again.

I suppose we would've continued into the wee hours of the night embracing the Goddesses' gentle swells if a mechanically amplified voice from the bluff overlooking Bull Head hadn't commanded, "Kayakers, come ashore at once."

It was the local gendarme. He judiciously informed us that because we had not left the park at sunset, we were libel to $84 parking fines. However, if we departed as fast as possible—and locked the gate behind us—it would only be a warning this time.

We locked the gate.

Stats

Distance: Who knows.
Speed: Ditto.
Time: Cut short.
Spray factor: Indescribable.
Dessert: Apple pie at Joe's.

15. Urban Kayaker

Remember the pilot for the original "Superman" TV series?

It was back in 1953, and George Reeves starred as the mild-mannered reporter / conscientious superhero. When the man-of-steel was dressed to fly, he simply lifted off the ground like a cupful of finely sifted flour and—light as a Grebe's tail feather—disappeared into the stratosphere (this light-footed technique appeared only in the pilot; in the actual series, getting off the ground turned out to be an overly expensive special effects boondoggle, and a cheaper but more belabored hop, skip, and a jump was adopted).

Thursday evening must've been our pilot because we floated away like a cup of sifted flour, too. Puff! Just like that, and we're airborne. One moment, the three of us are in the San Rafael Canal crossing under Highway 101 and the next we're drifting past crystal clear M.C. Escheresque can't-tell-the-top-from-the-bottom islands nestled in amongst the stars.

Had there been a hint of a wind down in the newly sculpted canal (part of San Rafael's flood prevention program), the islands we floated around might not have been as crisply textured. But there wasn't even a whispering breeze, and the absolutely still canal water mirrored our surroundings in surreal detail.

"Surreal" also might have been the dream of an elixir I brewed up and downed before our paddle. My back had been out of whack all week (due to cleaning bathrooms and toting large bundles of laundry—it's a guy thing), and I needed something to dull the gnawing ache. The herbal blend I concocted worked its magic, yes it did. Not only did I not feel any back pain, I felt no pain whatsoever. It was that good.

A little pain-relieving snake oil may be just the tonic you've been craving, too. So, in the spirit of the laissez-faire Goddesses

16. Storm Paddle

Thursday was a perfect day.

I had just finished carving a Greenland Storm paddle from the loveliest little piece of red cedar (straight grained, knot free, warm red), and the weather was howling and screaming outside my window. The storm Goddess evidently was beside herself with rage, twisting and shouting, her skirts flying, the rain doing a sideways blitzkrieg to match her every step. That little paddlea fist-width shorter than a regular paddlewas humming in my hands, let me tell you, itching to join the melee.

The Goddess must've heard my thoughts. A bolt of lightning straighter than the grain in that red cedar stick flew from her roiling eyes and lit up the living room. A millisecond later an angry roar slammed the house. The lights went out, the radio died, the computer monitor sliced to slate gray, and Sandy looked over from her desk and said, "You don't really want to go out in this, do you?"

That storm paddle sighed so loud I could hear it over my "No, no, not me" Rolfing of the truth. Another gash of lightning and grumble of thunder sealed the deal: me and the paddle were home for the duration.

Friday rolled out of bed with a gray hangover, but no slashing rain or screaming wind. That was the bad news. The good news was no lightning or thunder, either. I waited out the morningjust gray with a splash of rain.

"I think I'll go out and test the paddle now that things have calmed down, OK? Looks a lot tamer than yesterday."

This wasn't a question, either, but I kept my fingers crossed. The storm paddle held its breath.

"Be careful, and don't do anything foolish."

Yes!

I got to Bullhead Flat a little ahead of Gristle. I suited up, strapped my no. #2 stick to the foredeck, and launched into the bay with the storm paddle clutched in my hands. It was withdrawnbordering on depressedalmost from the first stroke. "This isn't a storm," it wailed, "this is only rain and wind. Look at that chop, hardly a whitecap out there. Swells not worth discussing. Don't taint me with this Shirley Temple water. I don't want any part of it."

"Shirley Temple?"

"Don't argue with me. Put me down."

"But this may be my only chance in a while to test you out."

"Frankly, John, I don't give a damn. Now, put me down."

Hard to argue with a high-strung, edgy paddle. It would've been futile, like trying to convince Rhett he really ought to stay with Scarlet at Tara. Fat chance. So I swapped the little guy for the longer paddle lashed to the deck.

Gristle and I set out in fairly benign conditions. The storm paddle had been right. A bit of a swell, but not many breaking caps. We were in a following sea, which made it kind of interesting, but not the stuff of storm paddles.

"Whataya wanna do?"

"Let's go out to that duckblind."

"Whataya wanna do now?"

"How about that other duckblind way over there?"

"Now what?"

"How about going over to Buck's?"

"You bring any money with you?"

"No, how about you?"

"Not a dime."

"We can get a beer later, right?"

"Sure, we'll get a beer later."

We paddled down a calm Gallinas Creek a ways past McGinnis Park, then turned around and headed back. "Shirley Temple Water." I was beginning to get the storm paddle's drift.

But we did plan something right this Thursday. We planned to leave Bullhead and flow with a flood tide, then head back on the ebb. And it actually worked that way (the stuff of Hollywood movies).

PBS (soon to loose its funding, I understand, along with the rest of the art world) has had a great series on the history of jazz. Totally and completely music challenged, I do have three sons who understand a bit of it, two who have actually spent quite a bit of time playing jazz. So I've been watching the series with some fascination.

The other night Wynton Marsalis, the great jazz trumpeter, was talking about Charlie Parker's immense contribution to the development of the genre, particularly as it evolved into bee-bop and pop music. Wynton was playing these magical selections from Parker, but he wasn't using his trumpet. He wasn't using any instrument.

"Doodly dot oh boogle chu rat tat tat
Pop doodly pop dot kachu daaaah
Dadadadadadada daaaaaah
(then he sucked both his lips in and made
a sound I can't reproduce here)
Foodly dooo shooo ooo mooo dooo
Plop flop dooododooodo

And so on.

Well, that stuff got sucked right into my head, and I couldn't get it out.

Until the return paddle to Bullhead Flat.

When the wind blows against a current, it tends to create larger waves than when it blows with the current. On the return trip, we had some nice sized water. The waves smacked the hulls . . . Pop doodly plop. Our bows would catch air, then smack down in the trough . . . Plop flop dooododooo. All the timein perfect timethe rain was pounding the deck . . . Dadadadadadada daaaaaah.

Bee-bopping on the water, that's what we were doing. At Bullhead, I went back out by Rat Island a couple times just to ride the tunes in, soloing most of the way . . . ka cha ka cha oodle dap doo.

Wynton doesn't need a trumpet, and I don't need a storm paddle (unless the beat really picks up).

Stats

Distance: Nine miles.
Speed: A good tempo
Time: 7/8s.
Spray factor: Every which way.
Dessert: Mooched a sweet maraschino cherry off the bar at Joe's when Ed the barkeep had his back turned . . . da daah.

17. Ray Gun

Jay showed up with his brand new, never-before-paddled Mariner. A gorgeous boat, right down to the same beaming yellow that radiates from my own Mariner's deck. Pups from the same litter, only a keen-eyed mother could tell our two boats apart. One subtle difference is my slightly older boat—first in the birth order—has more close encounters on its hull, but that situation should change soon enough.

Before we—Sam, Albert, Indiana, Gristle, Jay, and me—launched out of Sausalito's Schoonmaker Cove, Jay prestidigitated a bottle of bubbly from his rear hatch, and we solemnly baptized each of the Mariners. Sweet stuff, those baptismal waters. Following that little ritual, we indulged in the nautical sacraments ourselves, putting to rest the champagne and half a box of garlic-flavored crackers with a slug of humus.

The graph of today's tide was as flat as a rimless junkyard tire, sagging to a low of 1.4 feet at 11:30 AM and barely reaching 3.5 feet at 6:00 PM. It was a go-anywhere, do-anything tide. With the evening courting us in all its finery—just a spray of pancake makeup showing under its weathered skies—we set out for Angel Island.

Bisecting Richardson Bay and cruising up Raccoon Straits to Ayala Cove was like paddling across an accordion that's being squeezed together, the crossing happened so quickly. Time compressed, particularly when it's a sweet tune, isn't such a bad thing, and Jay the magician pulled a second bottle of champagne out of his bottomless hold for the song's finale.

After mimicking our pre-launch ritual on Ayala's soft beach, the six of us took to our boats. Though the Raccoon frequently morphs into dire straits, this evening's water was as blemish free as the long, skinny arms of a 20-year old model posing in a clothes catalog marketed to women twice her age. It didn't seem real, it was that perfect (generally, I pay scant attention to women's catalogs, though I do admit fancying Victoria Secret's glossy-covered wares).

We paddled straight across to Bluff Point on the Tiburon peninsula. Just before we reached the Point, two passenger ferries crossed paths quite some distance to our east, and we watched their distant tail-spun wakes trample the water before disappearing below the surface. Several minutes later, we caught sight of another stretch of water noted for its subsurface activities: Tiburon's WWII submarine base. Before we could explore, darkness turned us back to the straits and home.

Nothing unusual happened until Bluff Point.

This past week, a rather rare occurrence took place in a remote spot of water 100 miles off the coast of southern California. Wavessome of them 50 feet and higherrose up out of the water and careened along at 40 knots before dissipating. Scientists and extreme surf buffs say a slough of parameters have to line up like pigeons on a white-stained statue before waves of this immense size can form. Winds, tides, northwesterly storm swells, underwater land massesthat sort of thing.

You can check it out for yourself at this site:
http://dsc.discovery.com/news/briefs/20010129/surfing.html

Or this site (nice pics here):
http://www.swell.com/sw/content/mag/pulse/01_22_bank_one.jsp

It was pretty dark when we rounded Bluff Point, and I can't say for sure what I thought I saw was actually what I did see. But they looked pretty big to methose three waves up aheadlike three dark green Godzillas rising up out of Tokyo Bay and lumbering towards shore.

I paddled after the shadowy forms (having left my senses back by the submarine base). The creatures were big and slow, and I actually got to within mauling distance when they suddenly disappeared. Gone. Not a trace. Not a ripple, not a slimy scale. Just a breathless sigh floating on the water. Sent shivers up my spine, it did.

I have a theory.

As some footnote-worthy geologists may tell you, the isle of Atlantis, lying off the Marin coast, was subducted under the Continental Plate during a cataclysmic earthquake eons ago. Part of the island was scraped off to form Mt. Tamalpais with the remainder coming to rest 100 miles directly below Fresno. Bits and pieces also were deposited on Brook's Island over by Richmond. Something else was left buried in the Raccoon's mouth.

Here's what happened Thursday night:

The energy from those two long-gone ferry boats crept up to the Raccoon's mouth, then ballooned into the size of the Ghostbusters' Stay Puft Marshmellow Man with the assistance of a submerged ray gun. A ray gun designed by the clever Atlanteans. No doubt, the Great Subduction pushed the armed device deep down into the Raccoon's throat before it could be outfitted with a safety catch. Contrived to exaggerate mountains out of mole hills (the Atlanteans didn't have a mass media, just the ray gun), that pistola still functions, triggered by the merest of passing fantasies.

We really shouldn't be paddling in the dark.

Stats

Distance: Eight miles.
Speed: 2 knots.
Time: Four hours.
Spray factor: Not a factor.
Dessert: A slice of ice cream pie covered with a thick, rich mango syrup the owner of Avatar's in Sausalito served upgratiswhen he heard us mention Jay's upcoming b'day. Nice guy.

18. Ebb

Today was a big ebb tide, hustled along by the full moon. At 5.9 knots, it was almost as fleet footed as January's 6.0 knot full-moon ebb. Heavy duty storms kept us at bay last month, but no meteorological hijinks threatened today's free ride.

We launched from Gristle's secret bight just this side of Paradise. The ebb was already on the move, with the water visibly dipping away from the shoreline. Our free ride started right up, carrying the four of us around the nether regions of Tiburon to Bluff Point.

I was watching Sam round the corner at the point and head into Raccoon Straits. The ebb had been quick, and it wasn't unreasonable to think the current would make the turn and continue on its merry way toward the Golden Gate and Horseshoe Cove, our final destination.

What little we know.

The water Goddesses follow their fantasies, often confounding human logic and nautical charts. In this case, the ladies grabbed hold of Sam's boat and hurled him back where he had come from like a steel bearing launched from a slingshot. Kaaaawingggg. Fortunately for Sam, he was using his feather-light, hi-tech, carbon-fiber, black stealth paddle and managed to steer away from the rocky outcrop with a bag of fancy strokes.

Jay and I avoided Sam's redundant course by paddling wide before heading down the channel. Toward mid stream, we gave our paddles some R&R. Surprisingly, our boats stayed right where they were. No current to jostle them along. Not a hint of movement in the water. Sam and Gristle, on the other hand, were now about 50 yards to the north of us and battling against a stiff current running exactly opposite to the ebb. And three hundred yards to the south of us, the ebb was throttled up to full tilt and heading in the right direction, through the Gate and out to sea.

No figuring the Goddesses.

Except for Sam and his stealth paddle, Jay, Gristle, and I were using freshly carved Greenland blades. Eager to please, the sticks sliced through whatever the Goddesses lobbed our way. Wind. Water. Flying spray. The boards were dialed in and humming "Heave away, me jollies, heave away" (there're more lyrics to this little shantey, but they're too robust to repeat here).

Paddling a freshly carved Greenland is an adventure in aromatherapy, let me tell you. There's something indescribable about the smell of red cedar when it strikes up a relationship with salt water. Seduces the olfactory lobes, it surely does. You and your nose couldn't ask for a more sensual experience.

The paddle I had just whittled was a forest of olfactory delight. Almost as big, too. I'd used the entire length of an 8-foot board. Most Greenlands are around 84 inches long; this one was 96 inches. Truth to tell, it may have been more paddle than I had bargained for.

Bouncing in the chop with that Greenland humming old shanties reminded me of riding in a high-school friend's car. '57 Chevy. Stock . . . on the outside. Inside, it had a Paxton centrifugal supercharger forced induction system . . . Venola forged blower pistons, Crower rods with a magnefluxed crankshaft . . . 351 cubic inch SVO block with 4-bolt main bearing caps . . . Ford Motorsport GT-40 fuel injectors . . . Cyclone Tubular Racing headers . . . Koni gas-filled shocks . . . 3.55 rear-end ring and pinion gears. At 6500 rpm, that Chevy cranked out 600 horse power with 750 pounds of torque.

Now that I think about it, carving that skyscraper down a notch or two might be a smart move. Just to be safe. Big stick like that—if it got away from you—could cause a passel of trouble.

Two-thirds of the way down Raccoon, the ebb current kicked in again. Speeding out the strait's hind quarters, Sam shouts, "Do you think we'll be able to get around that breaking surf over there?"

Surf?

Sure enough, waves are breaking 150 yards ahead, the kind you can body surf on. Only there's no shore to scratch your belly on.

Just churning water. Like Mona Lisa's clever eyes, the image of these waves follows us no matter where we twist our heads. Inescapable, just like her smile.

But we have trump cards up our deck. Not only do our paddles charm their way through the frenzy, but Jay's and my new Mariner kayaks slice and dice that funny water like a midnight infomercial. And at no added cost, the glassed cockpits stay as dry as a fine Rhine wine. Call now, operators are waiting.

Sam didn't call, but he should have. He was on his sit-on-top and thoroughly drenched. Grinding him into the spit of fatigue, the Dolphin he captained was fidgety and had to be physically coerced through the chaos. By the time we finished the jaunt, Sam looked like he'd been run over and drug a nautical mile behind a large barge.

The kayakers who went the distance last month claimed the waters at Yellow Bluff—just north of Horseshoe Cove—were filled with wildlife: seals, birds, and fish of every description. No animals of any kind today. Just a giant, gray jelly fish floating in the sky, it's heart a yellow sun with dangling tendrils of black and purple clouds coalescing into foul weather, which—bless the Goddesses—waited until much later in the evening to dump on us.

We rattled our way through another patch of funny water before turning into Horseshoe Cove to celebrate trip's end. The flow in front of the cove's breakwater didn't seem like anything to signal home about, but as we watched from shore, a Coast Guard Cutter came sliding sideways across our field of vision at a nifty clip. Next to it was a sailboat that—without the Guard's help—would've headed out the Gate for ports-o'-call unknown to us. When the nose of the bigger boat faced the harbor's mouth, engines roared and the two vessels shot into the friendly waters.

That little dose of improv theatre really put a fine cap to the evening. Jay and I were on a high, and, after pouring what remained of Sam into my truck, we went to a little Indian restaurant in the backwaters of Sausalito for dinner. We watched Punjabi music videos with abandon, drank King Fisher beer, and hummed old sea shanties while the lyrics were still wet in our ears.

Stats

Distance: 8 miles as the gull flies, 10 miles up and down as the kayak bobs and weaves.
Speed: 5.9 knots on occasion.
Time: For one last King Fisher.
Spray factor: More than was necessary.
Dessert: Punjabi chocolate chip cookies.

19. Chocolate

Gristle eyes the metal strip jamming the channel. He flutters his hips to settle the boat in the water, tucks his head low between his shoulders like a loaded spring, and does something the six of us have never seen: the sexagenarian snaps his head up and bunny-hops the 17'6" long Pygmy Coho across the barrier.

Very cool move.

As a nation of kayakers, we're losing our paddling skills. I'm sure that in the dim, murky past, kids routinely kayaked bunny hops to impress parents and relatives. Trick moves like this, however, weren't just for show. No sir, not at all. They gave paddlers a boost in the keel when it came time to face the playful Goddesses.

And the Goddesses—if you haven't noticed lately—are plenty playful. Melting both the North and South poles, they are. Now, if that isn't a joke on us, I don't know what is. Acing bunny hops and other paddling basics may be what it takes to stay afloat in a world of rising liquidity.

To celebrate Wild Bill's b'day this Thursday, we (Wild Bill, Now-n-Again Ben, Sam, Jay, El Jacko, his buddy Michael from Italy, and yours truly) decide to hone our own basic skills and see if we can outsmart those wily Ladies. We set out from Black Point and head north up the Petaluma River. At Hog Island, we turn west onto San Antonio Creek. Though we didn't initially harbor the idea, a ways past the sleepy dock at Mira Monte we fantasize bringing home the proverbial bacon as a true test of skills. Real kayak hunting-gathering . . . providing for our families au primitif.

Lots of bird life in the water and surrounding marshlands: gulls, terns, herons, egrets, sandpipers, Canadian geese, an occasional hawk. Nearing the county's dump (a light nor'westerly alerts us to its presence way before we see it), gunfire erupts. POH POH. Then, WEEEE KAZAAAANNG. Wild Bill thinks it might be county personnel trying to civilize the gulls, but the noise only inflames the rowdy birds, who storm and squawk thunder above the piercing sound.

But we're not after birds; we've set our sites on bigger prey. Launching out of Black Point, we'd encountered a runabout of fishermen who had hooked a large sturgeon. It was a big fish, over four-feet long . . . a handsome meal to fill the most discerning gourmand. That's what we needed to impress the folks back home.

Wild Bill, the designated fisherman of our septet, hangs back scouting the waters for a likely sturgeon while the rest of us work our way past the dump's olfactory offerings. At a fork in the creek, we wait for Wild Bill. When he catches up, he claims to have seen the "ridged back" of a really big critter rise up next to his boat in the waters by the refuge heap. "Could've been a sturgeon," he says, "but the texture of the skin was all wrong." He'd never seen anything like it and let the shadowy beast lumber away.

Reunited, the eight of us veer off San Antonio Creek onto Woloki Slough and into the surrounding marsh in quest of recognizable prey. The slough—a narrow, twisty, convoluted affair—sucks us deeper into the marsh. The further we travel, the more it feels like the marsh is hunting us, digesting us. Satiated, it will eventually eliminate us like some offal mistake.

Deep into the miasma, we congest at a blockage in Woloki's alimentary canal, a stretch of corroded steel impeding our flow. El Jacko relieves himself of the tandem he's paddling with Michael and sets off in formerly new shoes across the marsh in search of an overland escape route. Gristle, in the meantime, ports his kayak over the steel constriction and paddles down the slough looking for a watery way out.

The rest of us wait. And wait. Then, we wait some more. No El Jacko, and no Gristle.

Scenes from "The Blair Witch Project" haunt our collective mind. Right before El Jacko wades through cobwebs into the dark basement of a deserted house, he returns to our group of five. He can see the Petaluma River nearby and thinks we could portage the boats over the marsh to it . . . if it weren't so dark. "Too many bog holes to risk breaking a leg," he says.

Some minutes later, Gristle returns, expertly bunny-hopping the steel stricture to say he thinks maybe we could exit up the slough, but since the skies are aging so quickly. . .

We retrace our strokes back to Black Point. It's a long, long haul, and we don't pull in under the big bridge until well after dark. On the way, we talk about food. The topic's all consuming, we're so hungry. For the last three miles, dark, soft ripples swirl off our bows, cast right out of that scene in "Chocolat" where Juliette Binoche stirs a vat heavy with sweet confections. Chasing that tasty and sensual illusion leads us to contentment.

As hunters, well . . . But as gatherers, we're still king of the food chain and spend the rest of the evening foraging at Joe's.

Stats

Distance: Way too far.
Speed: A couple knots, more or less.
Time: A little over five hours.
Spray factor: None.
Dessert: Chocolate-spumoni ice cream.

20. Yakity Yak

Yakity yak
and don't come back
   Robert Nighthawk and the Flames of Rhythm

"Where you wanna go?"

"I don't know. How 'bout the Sisters?"

"No way, not the Sisters. It'll be a pain; the tide's on the out, and we'll have to run quartering seas the whole distance. Forget it!"

"Yeah, well, we could ride the currents out to Red Rock, that'd be pretty cool. Haven't been out there in a long time."

"Gimme a break. The rips out there'll be ferocious and, besides, we'll be bucking the current coming back. It'll be way past dark before we see dinner."

"Ok, ok. How about we head down San Rafael Creek. Not much of a current there, lights everywhere, and lots of places to bail if we get hungry."

"Pedestrian."

"Dumb."

"Jeez."

"Boring."

They don't call us ka-yakers for nothing.

The five of us— Gristle, Sam, Albert, Jay, and me— float out Kong's portals at Bruno's on an ebbing tide in a barrage of indecisive chatter. The tree-sized poles guarding either side of the narrow opening are standoffishly rigid as we yap our way through.

Yakity yak. We talk faster than we paddle.

Albert's got a kayak trip planned for each month of the year, and we eat up his trip itineraries with a side order of jealousy and tossed envy.

Gristle's designing his own paddle, a cross between a Greenland and a white guy's stick, but he isn't divulging any details. We'll see it when we see it he says.

Sam can't figure out why we're even using 2 x 4's (not to mention closed deck kayaks) and pulls away from us with his hi-tech carbon fiber blade and Tupperware sit-on-top boat, tossing up more spray than we'll wipe off our faces all evening. We can only guess what he's chattering about up there, alone, in the distance.

Jay's on to some new kind of digital camera obscura, one that'll grab better pictures than his current fancy gizmo. The plentiful spray from Sam's boat is drifting down into my ears, but I think I hear Jay claim he'll be able to load the new camera's pictures directly into his Palm Pilot and beam them up to our email addresses while he's still out on the water. Ain't life great?

Me . . . well my paddle leash's all knotted up where I tied it to my deck rigging, and I can't finger the knots out. So I try to undo them with my teeth, but my tongue gets caught in the gnarly tangles. Before I know what's happening, I'm completely tongue-tied and can't add another sound bite to the evening's jabber. That's the solemn truth, if I could only swear it.

Truth aside, before we're able to decide on a destination, we arrive. We're in the ferry channel just south of San Quentin Prison, rush-hour traffic flooding the waterway. The tide's still a bit too uppity for stellar surfing, but it isn't bad, either. Being rush hour, there's an added tourniquet of pressure on us: lots of passengers— for lack of anything better to do— are eyeing us, waiting for a splashy upset or two.

We disappoint those eight-to-fivers, oh yes we do. There are no upsets, no tippy moves. After three or four flawless performances, we trundle back to Bruno's in high, dry spirits . . . when it starts to rain. Dressed for wet weather, we don't notice the downpour right off. The rain's visual, not tactile (except for Jay on whose hatless head mini water bombs raise a crop of tender welts).

Like tonight's rain, there's been a kayaker in our midst these many months who we didn't notice at first, but whose presence can't be ignored any longer.

BASK's Greenland paddling guru, Mike Higgins, put on a clinic at China Camp Beach Saturday to show what a 2 x 4 can do in the water. A couple days before the clinic, Sandy and I saw

"Crouching Tiger, Hidden Dragon." My kinda movie, let me tell you, people running up walls, flying over roof tops, dancing in tree tops.

At the end of the movie appears a list of people responsible for special effects. That list is longer than Rapunzel's ponytail, and the roster of techies who hid the wires lifting the actors to their fanciful heights was the longest. I looked real close for Mike's gravity-defying wires at China Camp Beach, but I couldn't find any.

That other paddler who's always been with us— but mostly unseen— was at China Camp, too, and he was visibly into the same trick moves. No hidden wires, no special effects. His name's Jack, and, even though we can see him now, when it comes to kayaking, we really don't know Jack.

Stats

Distance: Five miles.
Speed: Slower than chatter.
Time: 2.5 hours.
Spray factor: Only if you're near Sam.
Dessert: Irish Coffee at Joe's.

21. Bill Gates

I'm not one to judge seagulls, but this particular bird looked a bit like Bill Gates (might've been the eyes). Cornered all the good herring, too. He'd target a shadow slipping by just under the surface, then dive right through a melee of other gulls to capture his prize. Nearby birds would degenerate into a frenzy of squawking, but Bill paid them no heed, flapping skyward to chugalug his prey undisturbed.

The talented gull repeated this move over and over, rarely surfacing without a tender herring clamped in his shiny beak. Occasionally, one of the less able gulls would snatch a tippit off Bill's herring, but the better bird showed little concern, dismissing his underling with a charitable squawk.

Albert, Jay, Gristle, Sam, and I had launched out of Schoonmaker Cove into Richardson Bay in search of whales. Three had been spotted near the Dumbarton Bridge the day before, and we figured they might swim north into Richardson. We had played with a Gray here last year and were hoping for a repeat performance.

We didn't see any whales this Thursday, but we did come across a scene right out of the Discover TV channel: in the thick waters next to Sausalito's sewage treatment plant, a surge of sea life overwhelmed us. Seagulls, pelicans, cormorants, harbor seals, and sea lions. And the raison d'être for the get together: a matriculation of herring.

The birds— including Bill— paid us scant attention, but the seals and sea lions found us a curious lot. The sleek mammals followed us through the storm of feeding birds, eyeing us from one or two body lengths with rapt attention. They took a particular interest in Albert— maybe his deep blue and white kayak reminded them of a tasty marine treat (a blue-backed, white-bellied baskefer?).

Maybe not.

Jay and I did notice, however, that the critters showed a distinct preference for Albert's craft over our own yellow-decked banana boats. Perhaps being a vegan kayak in a sea of carnivores is a good thing.

The creatures followed us from one side of the feeding melee to the other, close to a nautical mile. For the entire way, the water was dense with ruffled feathers, flapping wings, splashing, and a mighty carping and screeching. The belligerent birds mixed it up beako a beako. Despite the rough play, it was an integrated, pc affair, cormorants and seagulls helping each other claw their way through friends and family for the tasty morsels.

The tide was at a standstill the entire time we mingled with the feeding hordes. No current to compete against, little wind to blow us off course, just a whimpering of gray rain. Rounding Yellow Bluff, the same calm conditions flowed under the Golden Gate Bridge and off into the distance toward the lighthouse on Pt. Bonita. Benign water under the Bridge is a rare sight, and we headed in that direction.

Crossing under the Bridge is a wonder, 1.2 miles of tinker-toy steel stretching from the Marin headlands to San Francisco. Squinting up the 220 feet from the water to the bottom of the span sets my head spinning (and, yes, the bottom of the bridge is International Orange just like the rest of the structure— though if the Navy had had it's way, the entire creation might have been striped black and yellow for better visibility).

About 600 yards west of the north tower sits Kirby Cove, where we landed on a stretch of red beach through a light surf. I'd heard there was a tunnel for exploring at low tide, but it kept itself secret, so we climbed the stairs up the cliff to explore the park, instead.

The place is enshrined in a grove of Monterey pines and eucalyptus trees and very green this time of year. The most prominent feature is the remains of a huge canon turret (sans the canon) on the edge of the cliff facing the straits. WWI? II? Earlier? Whenever, they really knew how to protect their parks back then.

We hung around in the rain for half an hour admiring the finery before shoving back out through the surf. Albert led the way with Gristle following. The old guy had a newly carved paddle (his own design— a cross between a Greenland and a European stick— whittled from a 2 x 6) that scooted him through the white soup like a seal through red herring. Pat. Pend.

The rain never stopped, and we were all pretty soaked by the time Schoonmaker loomed up. Jay, the most determined of us to Eskimo roll, made a few good practice attempts in Schoonmaker's small harbor, actually righting himself on one occasion. We were on the verge of applause, but he sheepishly admitted that he'd pushed off the bottom with his paddle.

But his attempt was game enough for us, and we celebrated the occasion with a few rounds of Taj Mahal beer at a fine little Indian restaurant deep in the interior of Sausalito.

Stats

Distance: Maybe 7-8 miles.
Speed: Adequate.
Time: 3.25 hours.
Spray factor: Only when the gulls and cormorants were duking it out.
Dessert: Apple-cherry crumb pie with a side of Punjabi chocolate chip cookies.

22. Barge

Lincoln, Charlemagne, King Tut, Wild Bill, Albert, Indiana. What do these folks have in common? Sadly, none of them showed up for Thursday's paddle.

I can understand why the first three didn't materialize, what with their heavy time constraints and all. But the last three—to a paddler, they chose nose grinding over kayaking. My oh my.

Speaking of my oh my, I've heard some Texans express concern over the energy "crisis" here in the Golden State. I say " " because it's really not so bad. Most of my paddling buddies simply cocoon themselves in their warm wet suits all day and don't suffer too seriously. There have been a few cases of frostbite and shattered digits, but according to Gristle, who expertly removed one of his own pinkies in a work-related mishap several years ago, you don't need all your fingers to fiddle a paddle, anyway.

Proving you can be a finger short of a full deck and still set the pace, the old guy guided our quartet—himself, Sam, Jay, and me—out of Bruno's into choppy seas and high winds on the flank of an ebbing current. Being his b'day, Gristle chose direction and destination: east toward the Sisters. Somewhat appetite challenged, we paddled out around Chard Island in hopes of munching some of it's dark green namesake, but the cupboard was bare and we continued on to the ladies.

Just past Pt. San Pedro and a half mile west of the Sisters, we locked our sights onto a passing tug-barge combo. The barge—a massive, floating steel box—was empty and sitting high in the water. The tug pushing it was no China tea set, either, but it was the large barge that fiddled a curious tune with my mind.

How could something that big and ugly float unassisted? Now, I understand a little something about volume, water displacement, and buoyancy, but when something that size crosses your wake, textbook physics just doesn't finger all the right chords.

To look at my pork belly, you'd logically figure I'd have a much better chance of staying afloat than that rusty, steel-walled monster. But toss me overboard without a life vest, and that's all the Goddesses wrote. Denser than a brass anchor, I am.

I'm not complaining, though. I understand that several of the Goddesses' young apprentices have, on occasion, mistakenly flooded the entire world, turned people into shakers of iodized salt, and placed humans high on a whale's list of recommended daily nutrients. If "to float or not to float" is the worse soliloquy the Goddesses can script for me, I'm not going to grouse.

While the four of us were busy pondering weighty imponderables, the two Sisters were preparing a surprise party for Gristle. When we arrived, neighborhood gulls plus several freelance Canadian geese kicked off the festivities by squawking a laudable "Happy Birthday" from the gals' white-laced, 24-hour Nautilus shoulders. Then the old ladies pulled out all the stoppers, and bubbly broke through the water's surface in a zillion mini geysers. Fine, sweet, intoxicating spray everywhere. The grandes dames just kept popping those stoppers like there was no end in sight.

A wet and wild mood stormed over us all. While the birds circled overhead and belted out original tunes, the four of us rock 'n rolled in the bubbling waters, dancing the boats from one end of the celebration to the other. Catching their breath every now and then, the Sisters would grab hold of the kayaks and spin them willy-nilly in dizzying circles across the wet party floor. All we could do was hang on to the gunwales and feel the spray in our faces.

Mere mortals that we are, we finally had to extricate ourselves from the white-frothed frenzy. Wasn't easy, either, those old gals popping stoppers, kicking up their heels, and grabbing at our parts. A half mile down the coast, we could still hear the revelers in full flow, ladies and birds rip-roaring right along with the last of the ebb under the bright light of a full moon.

Stats

Distance: Seven miles.
Speed: Way too quick for us.

Time: For just one more.
Spray factor: Up to the gulls.
Dessert: Went to Gristle's chateau after the paddle to continue the party on a human scale. His most lovely wife cooked up a feast of exquisite delectables, among them a bittersweet chocolate log that was indescribable. So I won't or can't (but it was v-e-r-y good).

23. North Sea

Eyes closed, heads lulling back and forth against padded couch ends, Sam and Jay flank the four of us—Gristle, Indiana, Albert, and me—like heavy-leaded book ends.

Tired to the bluff of exhaustion, Indiana is shivering so badly, he can't fall asleep. Albert, tireless and barefoot, is perched on the cushy sectional's ridge line, devouring every word and gesture offered by the white-haired British adventurer at the front of the room. Sitting resolutely next to Albert's feet, Gristle is mumbling loudly in tongues . . . Sanskrit, Aramaic, maybe Eubonics. I'm looking for an exit.

The six of us are at the back of the auditorium in the Haas Club House at UC Bezerkeley listening to a talk by the grandfather of modern sea kayaking, Englishman Derek Hutchinson. Derek is spinning tales about his first two attempts to cross the North Sea—a feat that had never been accomplished by anyone till he succeeded on his second try in 1976. The crossing lasted 31 hours.

Our little sextet has just completed a yo-yo to and from the Bezerkeley Marina and the end of its 3-mile-long pier. Our out-and-back took 2.5-hours. The dilapidated pier we paralleled points directly at the Golden Gate, through which ill-tempered winds and waves often come barreling through. This afternoon, both wind and waves are surly, but not as curmudgeonly as they could be.

The only boat in our pod that might have been upset by the testy conditions was my skinny, red-decked surf ski, paddled by Indiana. Ensnarled in a tangle of work the past few weeks, Indiana had been neglecting his kayaking, and this was his first outing in a moon of paddles. Had his skills suffered? The five of us watched with interest .

If it was Keystone Cops entertainment we were looking for, it didn't surface on the way out. Indiana and the ski were one.

Up the muddy little waves he'd scramble, 5 or more feet of the ski's exposed bow tilted up to kiss the wind before he'd leap off the crest and slap down into the following trough. Karrrroompf!

Repeatedly, without mishap.

At the end of the long pier, we did an about-face so that the nautical forces were directed at our backs, perfect conditions for surfing to the marina. Which we did . . . except Indiana. Sensing our growing displeasure with his paddling prowess and to reclaim his lowly position in the group, Indiana tactfully let the elements have their way with him. (An unwritten rule in the Solemn Book of Kayaking decrees a pod's least experienced paddler cannot upstage his seniors. A wise rule, indeed.)

Instead of slicing down the face of a wave, Indiana now let it pick him up, then spin him around on its crest like a toy propeller on a kid's beanie. Half the time, he'd skid backwards down the steep wall and stall at the bottom as the next surge of water broke over him. The other half, he'd simply fall off the boat. This was true Keystone Cops, and Indiana pulled it off with great aplomb.

Choosing between watching Indiana's performance and riding waves wasn't an easy decision, let me tell you. We finally ended up doing the democratic thing: we took turns surfing ahead, then paddling back to watch the show. It was great fun and the right thing to do. It also was exhausting. We were all blitzed by paddle's end, except for Albert who has an extra heavy-duty marine battery wired into his system.

From the marina's public dock, we went for a quick snack at the Sea Breeze Deli, then up to UC Bezerkeley to listen to Derek Hutchinson's tale. We were among the first to arrive and immediately usurped a big, comfortable aqua marine sectional in the back of the room.

Sam and Jay instantly fall asleep in their mountain of cushion. Indiana never warms up from his time in the bay and shakes uncontrollably during the entire presentation. While Gristle and I listen pretty attentively, Albert can't contain his excitement, kicking off his shoes and sitting on the top of the sectional for a better view of the speaker.

Gristle and I are rooting for Hutchinson to make the North Sea crossing on his first attempt, but unfortunately he doesn't. "Too bad," we think and are just getting ready to leave when the storyteller embarks on his second attempt. This telling is longer than the first crossing, and Gristle, who's been sustaining himself during the narrative by sucking bay salt off his moustache, starts to fatigue as the crystals grow thin.

The tale, eventually, is happily concluded with an entry into the Guiness Book of World Records, and we're ready to leave. But before we can stumble to our feet, the Englishman calls for questions, and Albert asks if there are any spots left in his masters paddling clinic the next day. With an adept storyteller's skill, Hutchinson seamlessly transports us to the Aleutian Islands, 70-knot winds, rats as big as wolves, and more high-seas adventures.

This is when Gristle starts mumbling out loud in strange tongues. There is no salt left to revive him. His moustache has been sucked dry. I look at the back of the room for an exit. There is one, but it's blocked by furniture.

Then, quite unexpectedly, one of the British adventurer's assistants gets out of his chair near the front of the large room and heads for a side door. As one—except for Albert who's wired for more tales—we shadow the unknown assistant from the room into a night warmed by distant oceans.

If our behavior was unruly, we apologize and blame it all on Indiana.

Stats

Distance: Six miles.
Speed: Two point eight knots.
Time: Two point five hours.
Spray factor: Heavy at times.
Dessert: Apple turnover and pecan pie, in that order.

24. Trickle Down

Until Friday night, the record for dilly-dallying the longest to purchase stuff was held by L B.—you know who you are—who, in 1984-85, spent 13 months actively shopping for a color TV before slapping his cash down on the countertop and walking off with the goods.

This evening, Sam showed up at Bruno's with a new kayak in tow. On the prowl for a sit-in since January 2000, it had taken him 3 weeks shy of a full fifteen months to exchange his cold, plastic Visa for a warm, dry boat.

A new record by a month and a half and reason to celebrate.

Jay brought beer and chips, and the three of us partied down in the parking lot to honor Sam's accomplishment. Janis Joplin's 18 Essential Songs blared from my truck's CD at Avalon Ballroom levels, pretty much guaranteeing that we'd have the space to ourselves. While Janis was belting out "Oh lord, won't you buy me a Mercedes Benz," the harbormaster did venture our way, but changed his mind mid-stride at "Prove that you love me, and buy the next round."

Gristle and Albert showed up during "Me and Bobby McGee," but Indiana was still a no-show, having cellphoned earlier to say he'd missed his ferry and would catch the next. We waited till Jay's big bag of chips was empty before giving up on Indiana and taking to the water.

Sam looked resplendent in his boat, a top-'o-the-line Nighthawk of genus Eddyline: 16' long,. 22" beam, retractable skeg, molded out of lightweight, nearly indestructible Carbonlite™. A well thought-out purchase, the craft's deck was the stuff of smiley faces, Slo Gin fizzes, and banana peels: a healthy, mellow yellow.

Just a tint-to-sunrise brighter than Jay's and my decks, that boat glowed.

Paddling three abreast, we skipped across the water like the Chiquita Banana Lady dancing the Macarena. Swinging around the northwest corner of Lesser Chard Island, the horizon-bound sun first pulled us one way and then the clump of islands to the east yanked us another. We were on everyone's dance card.

The only thing we could do was split the card, heading south across San Pablo Bay toward the Marin side of the Richmond-San Rafael Bridge and San Quentin Prison. On the way over, we scanned the horizon a time or two, but never caught sight of Indiana.

Crossing under the bridge, the big question was, "Whata we do now?" The parking lot celebration an hour behind us, the Trickle Down Theory of partying was beginning to have its effect, and we paddled to the nearest beach to empty our bladders.

Trickle Down is a major concern for kayakers. Aside from warming your wetsuit or jumping overboard to yellow the sea, the only sure way to combat TD is to keep land in sight. We've heard of several techniques to relieve the pressure while boat bound, but these usually require surgical implants or, if not, frequently disassemble into salty bogs inside the boat.

Fortunately, there's a public beach just around the bend from Pt. San Quentin. We left the kayaks on this sandy strip and headed for a cover of trees along the cliff's base. Blessing a tree is a simple matter since most wetsuits have strategically placed zippers. But not all wetsuits.

Mine doesn't.

To moisten the soil, I usually have to completely remove, in this order, my (1) life vest, (2) storm jacket, and (3) spray skirt. Then, I undo the shoulder straps on my one-piece wetsuit to peel the skin-tight fabric down to mid latitudes for a northern exposure. The whole process is fraught with buttons, zippers, Velcro straps, buckles, and belts. It's a nightmare of self-incarceration.

Jay, standing next to a neighboring tree, watches my slow striptease with a concerned look. "That takes too long, John, there's a better way."

"Oh, yeh, what's that?"

With the hand that isn't directing traffic, he pulls out a knife from the life vest he hasn't had to remove. "Here, use this," he says.

I take the knife and stare warily at the sharp, shiny edge. Visions of initiation rites on distant tropical islands dance across the blade . . . bonfires, slow beating drums, elders striking scalpel-sharp chips from dark blocks of obsidian, pods of scary-eyed youths in white loin clothes.A glint of cloudy sun off the blade startles me back to the beach. "Cut a hole in your wetsuit," Jay's saying.

That's a much better idea I think, and, without further consideration, I slice a deep, vertical line between two seams on my wetsuit's equator. I do a pretty good job, only dicing off a small square of bathing suit underneath. The rite completed, I honor the tree next to me, suit back up, and return to the water with the others.

Before heading back to Bruno's, we catch a couple decent rides off wakes from in- and outbound ferry boats. For the last pass, Albert paddles way out into the channel and latches onto a raft of water right off the next incoming boat's stern. He goes and goes and goes, and the only reason he doesn't surf further is because the ferry has to stop and let off its passengers. Pretty impressive for a kid from land-locked Orinda.

Chop, wakes, and TD finally behind us, we spy Indiana sipping beer at Bobby's Fo'c's'le. He says he arrived just as we were swinging out around Chard Island, and though he had the ski in the water, couldn't catch us in the chop. Figuring beer was better than paddling alone, he did his own loop round the islands, then returned to the restaurant to wait for us.

We chatter for a while, load boats onto cars, then move on to other ports where we test the limits of TD on dry land.

Stats

Distance: Seven miles.
Speed: Pretty good with passenger ferry assist.
Time: Two and a half hours.
Spray factor: Some going, none returning.
Dessert: We ate so much bread waiting for dinner, there was no room in the end for dessert.

25. Practice Makes Perfect

Leaving Horse Shoe Cove and scooting under the Golden Gate Bridge was a bit squirrelly, but nothing to upset our little mishap of paddlers—Albert, Gristle, Jay, Sam, and myself. The ebbing tide was a modest 3-point-something with headwinds peaking at around 5 knots.

We toyed with the idea of paddling a couple miles past the Bridge to Pt. Bonita Lighthouse, that white exclamation mark on the edge of the Pacific Ocean. But the further west the ebb took us, the nastier the water got. Half way up the Straits, we hung a U-ee and headed back to the Bridge. The choppy waters we sloshed through conjured up tales of memorable kayaking misadventures, which led to long-winded discussions of self- and assisted-rescue techniques.

The closer we came to the Bridge, the more raucous the water. It had morphed from a squirrel to a raccoon, battering us around like half-eaten pork chops under a park bench. We scampered every which way to elude the critter. Gristle cut left close to the tower and fought his way through a strong back eddy to the humbler waters of Horse Shoe Cove. Sam was to his right, churning through large swells before breaking free.

I was a couple boat lengths behind Albert, admiring how well he was handling his narrow-beamed, skittish boat. While watching him, I realized this was a Goddess-sent opportunity to practice the rough-water rescues we had just waxed so eloquently about. Capsizing and tumbling down the swell I was on would be an effortless affair, something I have a modicum of expertise in. And that's what I chose to do.

By the time I squiggled out of the boat and surfaced, the eager-to-play waters had drug me back down the Strait. I flipped the boat over and was trying to re-enter when Jay paddled up next to me, right on cue and textbook perfect. He caught hold of my deck to stabilize the boat, and I started climbing up the other side.

A flash of orange flew into my peripheral vision. I glanced up and spotted a Coast Guard helicopter hovering above us. An air rescue was not scripted into our practice session, and the fear of premature termination (not to mention the stiff rescue fees charged in the Golden State) catapulted me into the boat, lickety-split. Seeing my precocious skill, the orange bird flew off in search of other game.

With Jay still latched on, I began pumping water out of the kayak, careful not to reattach my spray skirt just to see what would happen. Sure enough, for every two gallons pumped out, a bucketful flooded back in. I waited until the kayak was 1/4 full before heading out under the Bridge again.

The water-logged kayak was less than stable, very difficult to handle. I started bobbing around like a buoy on a fishing line hooked to a 3-foot-long, angry steelhead trout. Up and down, back and forth, the water sloshing around inside the kayak like a storm in a bottle. With such perfect conditions, I again, with very little effort and modesty, plunged head-first into the murky water.

According to our well scripted game plan, Jay remained close by while Sam, Gristle, and Albert paddled into Horse Shoe Cove to practice reporting an incident. They waited until the Cove's two Coast Guard vessels had left on another errands of mercy before pretending to make their report.

In the meantime, Jay had stabilized both our boats by wedging his paddle under the webbing on my boat's stern, which made us rock solid in the bucking water. It was almost too easy to crawl back in, but we agreed it was a good learning experience and I re-entered the kayak. This time round, I reattached my spray skirt, then slid the pump down between it and me to empty out the water. No water leaked in while I pumped. I considered removing the skirt so the kayak could fill up—to make this simulation as realistic as possible—but my mind was beginning to fog, perhaps from cold and fatigue, and I left the skirt in place.

As we paddled out of the nasty stuff, a kayaker in a very narrow, very long surf ski approached us from the ocean side. We chatted. He seemed completely at ease in the funny water on his pencil-thin craft, bracing unconsciously every now and then to even his keel as he talked. Gravity by now had bought into our simulation, and I felt like I might fly off in any direction at any time, but watching the guy kept me grounded. When he took off for Horse Shoe Cove, I adlibbed some lines into our script and followed.

I actually got around the point to the Horse Shoe Cove side of the Bridge before I realized the folly of my misdirection. Making a mid-course corrective plunge, the current carried me back underneath the bridge to where Jay was impatiently waiting. I apologized for the slip, and we practiced another assisted rescue.

By this time, Albert had climbed from the cove out to the point and down some rubble to a tiny smidgen of sand. Pantomiming over the water's roar, he gestured us to get out of our boats and swim in behind them. But that was too easy, and besides, there was a rubberneck of tourists watching us from the walkway around the north tower. We couldn't go in, yet, not with an appreciative crowd watching.

Further up the Straits was a longer stretch of sand, and we headed for it. Timing the waves, Jay and I made a mad dash for shore. Twenty yards to go, a wave broke over us. Without thinking—too tired for that now—I again lost my place in the script and leaned into the white jumble with my paddle. The brace, unfortunately, worked, and I washed toward shore upright.

I could sense the crowd's displeasure. Fortunately, a sneaker wave saved the show, hitting us like an agitator washing machine, and tumbled both of us willy-nilly onto the beach. I could almost hear the rubberneckers' applause over the mayhem, and it warmed my chilled-close-to-hyperthermic heart.

We hung out to dry for 15-20 minutes. Feeding the gnawing hole in our stomachs had become an unanticipated concern, and Jay disgorged four big chocolate gingersnap cookies from his dry bag. Sweeter than Popeye's spinach, those hi-octane cookies were our cue to end the practice session. Spiked to the gills with sugar, we launched through the surf and paddled without incident back to the Cove.

Was our practice session a success? You don't have to be Ouija Board scientist to figure that one out. (1) My end-of-practice pale face replete with rock-star purple lips and bloodshot eyes, (2) the two AWOL lenses from the crumpled sunglasses dangling around my neck, and (3) our momentary status as a major tourist attraction say it all.

Stats

Distance: Three miles.
Speed: NA.
Time: 1.5 hours to go fifty yards under the Bridge.
Spray factor: Bigger than life.
Dessert: Chocolate gingersnap cookies, the best.

26. Root Canal

Shivering by the little concrete launch ramp at Bruno's, Indiana and I stared across the ruffled waters of San Pablo Bay, past Chard Island, out to the Richmond-San Rafael Bridge. It didn't look too bad, though the wind was snapping flags on boats like a leather whip in one of those B-rated porno flicks (I'm only guessing here, having never seen one of those specious movies myself).

Passing through Kong's gates—six upright telephone poles stuck in the mud on either side of the harbor's entrance—the wind kicked up immediately and heaved at our backs, a wonderful feeling, really. The tide was just beginning to flood and, with the wind lusting at the water, generous swells mountained up all around us.

Going with the flow of an unsettled following sea can be a complicated menage a trois for boat, paddler, and water, even downright discouraging at times. It's usually on the downside of a following swell that the water (and wind) can have their wicked way with your boat, twisting you hither and yon or simply stalling the boat so the wave in back can pounce.

The swells this evening turned out to be of good temperament, not overly complicated or discouraging. In fact, we managed to catch hold of a number of movers-and-shakers and surf them with relative stability.

Relative being the key modifier. More often than not, I had to stern rudder with my paddle to keep from broaching into a sideways slide. If I stuck the paddle too deep, the boat would slow and eventually stall, but with just the right amount of pressure on the rear blade, my rudderless kayak would embrace a wave and two-step quite a distance with it before disengaging. Indiana was hootin' and hollerin' somewhere close by, so I knew he was staying on top of things, as well.

We had set our sights on two Large Marge Barges doing earthquake retrofit work alongside the bridge, but the closer we got, the more agitated the wind and the rougher the water. With about 1/4 mile to go, we unanimously decided we'd gone far enough. The waters were becoming quite complicated, and if either one of us deep-sixed, the wind would push us to Never Never Land long before any thought of rescue would be possible.

So we did a 180. Well, Indiana did a 180. For the life of me, I couldn't get that kayak of mine to about-face. It would start to swing around, then a swell would lift the bow high and the wind would take hold and blow the boat back to it's original setting. I tried several times turning in the relative calm of a trough between two swells, but I couldn't do it fast enough. I even tried paddling backwards in the trough to keep the bow down and out of the wind, but to no avail.

The wind blew me 1/8th mile off course before I struggled through a brief lapse of inattentive breeze. Back on course, Indiana and I did head butts with the wind before we found shelter on Chard Island. We waited there until the sun was nearly down, then shoved off. Without the inferno stoking the air, we finished our paddle in relative calm.

Heaped on top my prolonged swim under the Golden Gate Bridge last week, this recent inability to turn things around had shoved my confidence to the brink. Warming our frozen hands around big mugs of steaming chocolate at Bobby's Fo'c's'le later in the evening didn't help, either. I acted cool—like I had everything under control—but I didn't. Of course, I couldn't let Indiana or anyone else know. Being male is tough.

Fortunately, I'm not a single-sports person. No, siree, I am not. I'm a biathlete. Besides kayaking, I'm also an Xtreme Napper. And two days after my disappointment in the bay, I achieved a certain accomplishment in Xtreme Napping that has restored my confidence. Big Time.

I was in the endodontist's chair for a root canal at 7 AM. In itself, a root canal is not necessarily a confidence builder. No matter how you look at it. At this particular time, I wasn't looking at anything, my eyes squeezed shut while the good doctor stuck an incredibly long and crooked piece of metal into my jaw. To numb it he said, but I knew better.

Numb is numb only when it's numb. That piece of metal found it's pointy way into my tender gums four separate times before the promised numbness took hold. Then the doctor says, "this is one heck of a complicated tooth" and "has it settled down, yet," and I start making word associates and end up fussing about that paddle two days ago. Whatever smidgen of confidence is still clinging to me has just stuffed its dry bag and is shimmying out through a porthole when an amazing thing happens.

The endodontist is on my right, chiseling away by hand on my tooth with a jagged rasp. I've seen photos of similar devices in National Geographic articles on the Spanish Inquisition. Scraping against the inside of my tooth, it sounds like a chain saw with a clogged carburetor. I can't feel it, but I can feel it, you know what I mean. To my left is the doctor's assistant, a pretty young thing who is pregnant. Very pregnant. Her baby, due in a month, is kicking my shoulder as hard as she/he can. Over and over. I have tendinitis in that shoulder (if not before, certainly now).

Pulling out all the meager reserves I have left, I dig down deep and find new strength: in the turmoil of the chair, I fall asleep.

The doctor wakes me up because I've taken a bite out of his finger. I'm stunned. I can't believe what's just happened. Not since Ronald Reagan dozed off during critical negotiations with the Russians over nuclear weapons in space back in '86 has an instance of Napping Under Duress been documented.

I nap and bite several more times over the course of the procedure. I'm really on a roll. If only officials from the Xtreme Napping Federation had been present, I might've qualified for the national team right there and then.

Now, don't get me wrong. I would never claim to be on a par with Reagan—the only napster to have ever reached the black belt of napping with a 10th degree title of "Yapper Dapper Napper"—but I must admit that this root canal has been encouraging. Very encouraging.

My confidence is back.

Stats

Distance: 4.6 nautical miles.
Speed: 1.84 knots.

Time: 2.5 hours.
Spray factor: All over.
Dessert: Fresh key lime pie with whipped cream.

27. Whims of Chance

The old wood dock in front of Buck's hadn't ever been much to gawk at, just a mismatch of uneven boards strung together with rusty nails. But you could line up a slough of kayaks along it's length for en masse put ins. Not any more.

A real howler must've torn it apart sometime during the last two weeks. Dismembered, it was. All but one ancient segment had been plundered and tossed into the tule grass like discarded bait. What was left could barely handle two kayaks at a time.

Squeezing onto the battered raft, Sam and Gristle slipped into Gallinas Creek first, then I followed. Avoiding the carnage altogether, Indiana and Truckee Steve—visiting the Bay Area for the weekend—launched from the adjacent concrete ramp.

A kid-sized westerly raised some waves on the flooding tide, but we were able to paddle through the chop without much trouble.

This was Truckee Steve's first time on Gallinas Creek, so we gave him le grand tour: west out of Buck's toward the freeway (four miles distant) into a swelter of Popeyesque houses on the creek's south side; on the opposite shore, acres of pristine marshland. Past the spinach-inspired Fleicher Studio homes, the waterway narrows to a boat width. Once five abreast, we're now single file, paddle blades digging into the muddy banks, an occasional mallard or tern helicoptering into the sky.

After a half-hearted but lengthy run, the creek empties into a quarter-mile-long storm drain that skirts under Highway 101. Sitting on top a 4-foot tide, we follow Truckee Steve into the black hole (if it's your first time, tradition dictates you lead the parade). Lights are forbidden, our positions in the dark tunnel marked only by paddle splashes and animated conversation bouncing off slick concrete walls.

The storm drain is 10 feet across, and those of us with long boats can't turn around at the far end. After paddling out backwards for a quarter-mile, Gristle maneuvers his kayak in the creek so Indiana—who's climbed off his sit-on-top and is wading knee-deep through the cloudy water—can pick up the bow and spin him around on his stern. Unfortunately, Steve's boat and mine are a bit too long to take advantage of Indiana's muscles, and we back-paddle another quarter mile till the creek widens enough for us to do an unassisted 180.

A mile from Buck's, the channel splits, one arm rippling out to the bay and our cars, the other wrapping around in the opposite direction to the northwest. We follow the latter to a healthy little dock that has survived the winds far better than its geriatric relatives at Buck's. This little pearl of a boat rest is within walking distance of McGinnis Golf Course and The Club restaurant.

The last time we graced The Club with soggy wetsuits, paddles, and rubber booties, we'd been less than enthusiastically greeted by the restaurant's well feted patrons and had left before we could dribble beer on the carpeted floor. But that was then and now is now, so we decided to give the establishment another run for our beer money.

The Club's good fortune, however, was our misfortune—though we were outfitted with hand flares, smoke bombs, and small rocket launchers (at the ready for open-water rescues), we lacked cash—and were forced back to Buck's in a surly, thirsty funk. Buck's was home to the goods we needed, but had latched its shutters hours before.

And that's how the evening would've ended, but the Goddesses were looking out for us, and the whims of chance blew us into a little eatery under the overpass at the end of Fourth Street in San Rafael. There we ran aground against mounds of good food, which we promptly washed down with bottles of cold, imported beer.

Stats

Distance: Nine miles.
Speed: Faster forward than backward.

Time: Two point five hours.
Spray factor: Insignificant.
Dessert: Rafting up in the middle of Gallinas Creek after exiting the storm drain, Indiana passed around creme-filled cookies and Truckee Steve tossed us each a chocolate Easter egg. Since Gristle wasn't into sweets, I ended up with two eggs in my bread basket.

28. Hawaii

Sandy and I just returned from a week in Honolulu. Except for having to leave the island, it's nice to be back.

As vacations go, it was pretty good, but not 100% carefree—unless you call chaperoning 78 high school students carefree (the kids were competing in a music festival when they weren't swimming circles around us). Chasing after that many kids is like paddling into the wind against a strong current in confused seas. Without a paddle or PFD. Just tow ropes. Fortunately, 18 other parents were in the same leaky boat with us, and we all took turns capsizing.

Except for the winds, Oahu was a nice change from the Bay Area. It was warm—in the mid 70s to low 80s—and the ocean wasn't too many degrees off that. Although Honolulu is a huge Tourist mecca with a capital T, the pace there was decidedly slower than here. Lots of public transport to go hither and yon, though, judging by the crowded sidewalks, I suspect most folks hoof it within the city's confines when they can.

Didn't see a single kayak. That was a disappointment. Outside of a hundred trillion surfers, I did spot a few slender outrigger canoes. Most were for multiple paddlers, a few for singles. The longer boats are available for rent all along Waikiki Beach, and each is outfitted with a guide. They don't venture too far out to sea, just far enough to get beyond the surf zone (anywhere from a 1/4 to a 1/2 mile). Then they come roaring back to shore, hitch-hiking on waves through the brightly coraled shallows.

Surfing the outriggers looked like a lota fun, but I never got beyond the looking part. The boats were either in use or the guides were tuckered out when I tried to part with my money. Sandy and I finally did succeed catching a ride on a catamaran late in the afternoon of our last day on the island.

The ride turned out to be more fun than we anticipated. The water within the surf zone is relatively calm (the winds from the other side of the island scoot over the steep interior mountains and touch down well beyond the furthest breakers).

Once the catamaran got into the windswept water, the waves more than doubled in size. Tacking directly into them, the bow of our boat would rise high up on a crest, then slide down the face into the sinking trough. Egged on by it's momentum, the catamaran's broad nose would punch into the advancing wave's leering face and, as the native's say, "surf's up."

One tanned young lass hanging onto the shiny railing next to us was sipping a pink mai tai cocktail just before we submarined through the first wall of water. When we ploughed out the other side, her drink had been replaced with a salty green margarita, if you can believe that.

The waters closer to shore weren't bludgeoned by the howlers and would've been ideal for kayaking. Clear, warm, mellow. Struggling in the gusts where we were would've been a different story. While the waves weren't too confused—they behaved like well trained soldiers, all marching in orderly lines—the hefty breezes really set things spinning, whipping white caps into wildly sculpted meringue toppings.

Paddling might've been doable, but just barely for me. After my flounder under the Golden Gate Bridge a couple weeks back, my appreciation for the water's whimsically strong personality is on the upswing. Cranking up that respect a notch or two was a mishap of long-time, skilled kayakers getting pummeled under the bridge a short week after my own misadventure (the Coast Guard had to dive in and rescue the unfortunate crew).

If you really want to develop a healthy respect for the water (without having to stick your toes in), read "Deep Trouble." Wild Bill loaned me the book to peruse during the trip. Devoured it is what I did. Nearly drowned in it's tide rips and turbulent prose. That's one tome you're better off reading after you've learned to Eskimo Roll.

Speaking of deep trouble, don't ever let your wife catch you ogling the scanty swimwear on Waikiki Beach. If those monosyllabic swim suits were words in an email message, the new fangled internet filters would never let them through. Which explains all those cold showers up and down the beach. When I first got to Waikiki, I wondered why they had so many. Now I know.

Swim suits and cold showers aside, the San Rafael High School kids we were chaperoning were hugely successful in their music endeavors. Besides winning a heap of trophies between climbing up Diamond Head and snorkling in Hanauma Bay, the Jazz Band won the Best of Show Grand Prize. Not too shabby.

Stats

Distance: 4,000 miles.
Speed: 562 mph.
Time: Uncomfortably compressed in those wedged-together airline seats.
Spray factor: Outside the surf zone.
Dessert: Too numerous and tasty to describe.

29. Shakespeare on the Bay

The Goddesses are like little kids with big magnifying glasses. Once they get a tangle of light unsnarled and focused, the water really begins to boil and bubble.

We'd planned to launch out of Horseshoe Cove, but I got a call from Jay crossing over the Golden Gate Bridge earlier in the afternoon. "The wind's rocking my car side-to-side," he shouts into his cell phone, "and the bay's loaded with white caps. Gulls heading into the wind are barely moving, but ones going east are Cruise Missiles. You sure we wanna put out of Horseshoe?"

There's no debate. Instead, we meet at Schoonmaker Cove in Sausalito at 5:30 PM, just a couple miles north of Horseshoe. For kayakers, those are important miles: the headlands separating bay from ocean along that stretch act like the Great Wall of China and repel invading westerly winds.

Five of us—Jay, Gristle, Sam, Wild Bill, and I—aim our boats out the cruiser-lined mouth of the swank little harbor (Larry Ellison of Oracle fame parks his white ocean liner at Schoonmaker, usurping quite a few good-sized berths in the process). Just to see how bad conditions really are, we decide to ply southeast across Richardson Bay toward Angel Island, which lies in the direct path of any nastiness passing through the Golden Gate. If what we see doesn't suit our genteel tastes, we'll do an about face, back to calmer waters.

Bay weather is a one-person Shakespearean stage play, with frequent costume and mood changes. By the time we near the southwest corner of Raccoon Straits, what started out as a mad, unkempt Hamlet has cross-dressed to a well-behaved, pleasantly attired Cordelia. Just a light breeze at our backs and 50 yards of rip tide to scramble through before sliding into the channel proper.

A piece of Elizabethan cake.

We paddle up a head of steam to cross the eddy line separating the sedate water from the faster moving rip. Can't help but get spun around a tad by the excitable water, but we're able to keep our bows pointed more-or-less toward Angel Island.

Though the more quarrelsome winds are taking a breather, the Goddesses are still playing with those magnifying glasses, cooking up trouble at the head of the channel. Wind fetches unobstructed from the Bridge to Raccoon Straits, and good-sized wind waves can build up quickly. Especially if the gusts are blowing against the tide, which they've been doing this afternoon.

Fortunately, the waves aren't jammed together, and we have plenty of room to recover after each surge passes. Even though boats and paddlers frequently drop out of sight behind mounds of water, conditions aren't nearly as demanding as the Goddesses' performance of "The Tempest" three weeks ago under the Bridge. In fact, after the first unruly waves thump and shutter under us, we find our sea legs and manage to surf the tamer swells toward Angel Island.

A small spit of land juts into the straits on the windward side of the island just before a little stretch of beach. Fifty yards from shore, the surface turns mirror smooth, and we glide out of the still water onto tawny sand. To our right a set of steps carved into the hillside switchbacks up the cliff through a grove of eucalyptus trees. At the top, a green meadow opens up like a flower, replete with barbecue pits, picnic tables, level camp sites, and views of the Golden Gate Bridge and the north end of San Francisco.

An official state park sign proclaims, "Kayak Camping."

Just when you think you know all there's too know (been there, done that), you stumble across a little pearl like this one tucked away in a public oyster. Visions of sugar-plum brandy, camp fires, roasted marshmallows, and overnighters dance through our collective fantasies just as twilight starts its last gleaming, and we descend to beach and boats.

Still talking overnighters—we talk party more frequently than we party party—we launch back into the quiet alcove and paddle out into the last of the evening's jumbled waters at the Raccoon's mouth. Direction is now our strength, and we paddle into waves, which is far easier than running from them. Just outside the mouth, the rip slows to the pace of a grocery store conveyor belt and, within a few minutes, deposits us in the middle of a mellow Richardson Bay.

Half way across and 1/4 mile to the west, a spout of water snorts skyward. A swath of black crests behind the geyser, and we catch our first glimpse this year of a bay-bound gray whale. Eager to see more of it, we hang 1/2 mile off shore directly across from Sausalito's water treatment plant where grays frequently dine on the nutrient-enhanced bottom.

Half an hour passes without another sighting, and we decide to call it an evening. Near the opening to Schoonmaker Cove, we unexpectedly tack into Indiana's wake. He couldn't sneak away from work until late, missed our launch, and has been paddling by his lonesome. Alone but not entirely unhappy: he's in his new kayak—a Mariner Express—with an equally new, super lightweight graphite paddle in hand.

The sight of Indiana's new, sleek boat and aggressive paddle causes whatever testosterone we have left to seethe and boil. Someone in the group challenges him to a race . . . from here to the red-striped buoy way over there. We line up, paddles nervously slapping water. Wild Bill trumpets, "Vamos," and we're off.

When the results are in, it's pretty clear: old guys are better off drinking beer. Which is how we spend the rest of the evening, drinking beer and trying to catch our breath.

Stats

Distance: Eight miles.
Speed: Four knots.
Time: Two hours.
Spray factor: Only in the Raccoon's mouth.
Dessert: Apple pie and chocolate chip cookies.

30. Goddess R&R

The little dribble of sand at Schoonmaker Cove is awash with kayakers when we arrive at 5:30 PM. Most are part of a Sea Trek class just returning from a jaunt on Richardson Bay.

"Windy out there?" we query (as if we don't already know, the gusts playing a wild Brahm's concerto on the rigging of nearby anchored boats).

"Pretty heady," the paddlers reply.

Our plan is to travel south along Sausalito's swank waterfront, hugging the hi-brow Armani shoreline to keep out of the pesky wind. Six of us—Jay, Gristle, Sam, Indiana, Adam's Dad (his first outing in the bay with us), and I—saunter past the backside of Sausalito's finest in relatively benign and uncrowded waters.

The streets just a few kayak-lengths away are flooded with people and cars—not because of pre-Cinco de Mayo festivities or "Everything Must Go" sale-a-thons. No, indeed. It's a commuter's worst nightmare out there: 12 miles north on the main escape route (Highway 101), a car is/was on fire. Bumper-to-bumper takes on a new, heated meaning.

While northbound commuters do a slow simmer in their gridlocked vehicles, we amble toward the water treatment plant on the south end of town just this side of Yellow Bluff. Jay's Chief Mate spotted a whale in the vicinity while sculling earlier in the morning (she's sited whales every morning since last Friday), and we hope to duplicate our own close Cetacean encounter of last week.

"Whoa!" (or some such Barbary-Coast expletive) shouts Sam, "look at that back eddy." The waters just ahead of our own calm seas are roiling, jetting out a good fifty yards into the bay. Just when you think you've outsmarted the Goddesses or caught them napping, they slip one by you. However, on closer inspection, the eddy is not the work of the Goddesses, but a warning sign from the Golden Gate Transit District. Hidden from our view, a passenger ferry is revving up it's twin engines, readying itself for San Francisco.

We consider a mad dash across the narrow lane before the big boat backs out, but wait a skosh too long and watch the ferry's southbound wake roll on without us. Before we can commiserate our surfing loss, the nearer northbound wake scrunches under us and tosses us a bit this way and a bit that way. Entertaining, but nothing like the Goddesses' handiwork.

Shortly after crossing the ferry's path, the water paralleling the shore begins to kick up its heels without any mechanical assistance. We're at the south end of town, where breezes that whip past the gate and curl around Yellow Bluff often butt heads against gusts coming down from Sacramento 90 miles away. Brahm's again, but with a much larger wind section.

Several of us want to go back to the tamer concerto at Schoonmaker. A few want to head across Richardson Bay towards Angel Island, where it doesn't look so confused (at least from where we're floating). Those favoring Schoonmaker have already turned and are heading back. The rest of us give chase. During the pursuit, the winds have straightened themselves out and are now blowing uniformly to the east. We raft up and discuss our evening's options. Indiana, who's been acquiring new toys, brings out his latest: an almost-waterproof, handheld GPS unit.

Besides charting in real-time our squiggly course on its phosphor screen, the electronic gizmo also calculates our total distance, average speed, and current speed. "Look at this," says Indiana, "we're clocking 2.5 mph right now." Which is pretty good, since none of us is paddling. Wind and a steady flood tide are finally conspiring to help us.

Being a resourceful group, we let the Goddesses make the rest of our travel plans and float across the bay to Belvedere. By our arrival, the winds have been coddled to passivity and the bay is well behaved. We paddle along the steep coastline, admiring the stately estates perched on wooded cliffs, some pretending to be Mediterranean palaces, other aspiring to Tuscan villahood, while a few are a patchwork quilt of the most fashionable.

We skim the entire length of Belvedere before heading back across Richardson for Schoonmaker. With his GPS, Indiana picks out a direct line. It's too direct, and we come up to the little harbor's entrance before darkness.

"It's too early to take out," I protest. "Let's paddle a bit longer."

His stomach audibly yodeling, Jay's more inclined to dinner, but offers a compromise: "Let's see if the Cruising Club is open and get a few snacks."

Cruising Club?

Leading us through a confusing maze of ships, yachts, and docks, Jay deposits us in front of a long building rocking on a barge. "Cruising Club" is carved across its plain front. We anchor our kayaks to a friendly dock, hike up a flight of steps, and knock on a wood-framed door. An older fellow appears and asks for our membership IDs.

Membership IDs?

"You gotta have membership IDs to get in," he explains.

We admit to a lack of membership IDs and reluctantly head back down to our boats.

Before we can launch, the fellow returns to the door and shouts down to us, "The ladies want to know if you belong to any other clubs?"

Quick as a sculling brace, Jay shouts back that he's a member of a yachting club up at Tahoe.

"Well, then," says the guy, "come on in."

Inside is a single long room. Running half it's length is a highly polished wood bar. Sitting straight-backed at the bar—flanked on either end by two white-haired gentlemen—are seven ladies of distinctly strong personalities.

"Paddling kayaks, are you now?" observes one.

"Your friend's stomach's growling," says another and two baskets of munchies materialize in front of us.

"You'll be wanting drinks, too," says a third. Looking at the barkeep, "Ask the boys what they want."

We order drinks. Jay orders a bourbon and seven; when the drink arrives, it's missing that warm tan the back hills of Kentucky are famous for. One of the silver-haired gals silently eyes the barkeep, and he says, "Oops, forgot the bourbon," and replenishes Jay's glass without comment.

The ladies, all a level or two of maturity beyond us, keep to themselves at the shiny bar, animatedly discussing matters of apparent consequence. The men don't interfere in their conversation. Occasionally, the women glance our way and suggest more snacks and drinks.

When darkness cozies up to the Cruising barge, we take our leave and start a lazy retreat to Schoonmaker. As we're about to push off the dock, one of the guys comes out to say good night. Before he can head back in, I ask, "What're those old gals up to, anyway?"

"The Goddesses, you mean," he says with a nervous twitch to one eye. "Regular forces of nature, they are. They come in here every now and then for R&R and to make plans, or so they claim. Don't ever want to upset them," he adds, "they can kick up quite a storm if you're not mindful," and he saunters back into the dimly lit building, latching the door behind him.

"Now, whataya think he means by that," I turn to ask the others, but they've already paddled off. "Goddesses, huh? I think the old guy's had too much to drink," but a sudden gust of purposeful wind slaps the paddle out of my hands, suggesting otherwise.

Stats

Distance: Seven miles.
Speed: Pretty good for not having to lift a paddle.
Time: Six hours if you're using Indiana's GPS, which is set on Eastern Standard Time.
Spray factor: Only when you upset the Goddesses.
Dessert: Bourbon and seven with real bourbon in it.

31. Tropical Terrarium

With daylight stretching her long, pale legs into the evening hours, we pushed the launch a half hour past our usual summer time to 6:00 PM. Black Point (under the overpass on Highway 37) is more than a few miles to our north, and we left San Rafael just before 5:30 to reach the public ramp on time. Typically, Highway 101 heading north is a thick bog of frustrated commuters, but tonight it was almost car-free.

Getting to the freeway from my house was the problem. Gristle and I carpooled in his '82 Datsun (a.k.a. Nissan) pickup truck through a slough of downtown traffic. San Rafael is in the midst of raising high the roof beams on it's midtown revitalization, and construction crews and blocked-off streets have gummed up traffic. Compounding the slog, most of Fourth Street Thursday nights is turned over to an outdoor Farmer's Market, which really puts a damper on exiting the city.

Fortunately, driving the 20 miles to Black Point from the highway took less time than stitching together the two miles from my place to the freeway on ramp. We jockeyed into the launch just as Wild Bill and Sam were unloading their boats. Dave from San Francisco also was there. A first timer, he was in the painstaking midst of choosing a new kayak, and a Mariner Express was on his short list. Indiana—in a true gesture of midwestern hospitality rarely seen in this Golden but sometimes Tarnished State—had volunteered to let Dave test the waters in his brand-new Express.

Unfortunately for Dave, Indiana had cell-phoned earlier, claiming he had taken to heart the Administration's conservative ethic of nose-to-grindstone and was staying late at the office for patriotic reasons. Fortunately for Dave, I had lugged along an extra kayak for Ancient Bob who did a no-show (we later learned the old geezer went to the wrong put-in, but that's understandable for a guy who carbon-dates as far back as he does), and Dave was able to paddle with us despite Indiana's work-a-holism.

Our little pentagon—Wild Bill, Sam, Gristle, Dave, and I—paddled straight across the channel and eastward up a little tributary past a two-penny yacht harbor. The harbor was snoozing and the tributary dead-ended less than a half mile beyond. We gawked at a few birds pecking in the mud along the ropy bank, then decided to venture out into the bay where more birds were reputed to hang out.

Rounding the dimpled mouth of the channel and facing the bay, we were greeted by a frisky wind. Unlike the gusts that have hammered us in weeks past, this little gal was real friendly and fun-loving, kind of like Marilyn Monroe in "The Seven Year Itch" (the one where a hoot of wind from a sidewalk grate billows out the blonde's revealing skirt). A real delight.

The playful breeze had fetched unimpeded across the bay from Vallejo and stirred up a welter of 1-2 foot high waves. Our next move really wasn't a tough choice: either hug the waveless shoreline to admire the wildlife or get the old adrenaline flowing in the cushy spray. Heading out into the watery amusement park offered up another advantage: it gave Indiana and his speedy vessel a chance to catch up to us (Indiana, realizing he wasn't as conservative or patriotic as he imagined, had taken off from work earlier than planned).

Plying into the wind and chop was a splashy affair. The evening was south-seas balmy, and I loosened the top of my tight spray skirt to let trapped body heat escape the cockpit. Within a stroke or two of unleashing the waistband from my chest, a snappy wave broke over the boat's bow and slopped down the opening into the cockpit. Over the course of the evening, buckets of waves groped their slippery fingers down my front to dampen the kayak's interior. But it wasn't a chilling experience, no not at all, the water almost as tropically warm as the night air.

A bathysphere of warmth is what it was out there, a regular equatorial terrarium. After a mile or two of churning through mild spray, we turned the boats around and surfed the little windwaves back toward Black Point. The wavelets were just the right size: not big enough to overpower the kayaks nor so small to stall the boats out.

We cruised along for the longest time, leaning this way and that to cut a straight line, before Wild Bill suggested we raft up and indulge ourselves in food and drink. The feasting table was wide, six boats crowded together, gunwale to gunwale. Some of us pulled out vials of magic elixir from the damp interiors of our boats, others silvery-wrapped trinkets of food. It was a scramble passing vittles across decks, and the level of excitement rose to a feverish Gilligan's Island pitch.

With the energy level cresting, Gristle reminded Indiana that he had invited Dave to test his Express. That we were still bobbing in the bay didn't scuttle the exchange in the least: floating on either side of our banquet table, Indiana and Dave crawled out of their respective craft, scurried across the four intervening decks, and slid into the other's kayak. It was a genuinely impressive sight to behold.

With a well shaped ankle of daylight left, we paddled away from Black Point toward Bel Marin Keyes. Half way there, Dave announced he had to get home, and Indiana followed him back to the launch ramp. The rest of us paddled on until we didn't feel like paddling any more, then turned around to face the distant overpass and our unseen vehicles. With a friendly night wind licking our backs, we rafted up again and let the Goddesses push us along, paddles lifeless on our decks.

While we lollygaged towards our parked cars, a spontaneous aerial show of impressive proportions took to the air. They were too high and dark in the night sky to identify, but wave after wave of birds—zillions of 'em—in tight V formations would rush downwind, then abruptly careen head-on into the breeze and plump out in all directions like Marilyn's spirit-lifting skirt. The performance spiraled on and on until it got so dark we couldn't see any more, which was a shame because it's such a good movie.

Stats

Distance: Seven miles.
Speed: Heady with the breeze at our backs.
Time: Not enough daylight.
Spray factor: More going than coming.
Dessert: Little itty-bitty cookies and apple-cherry Clif Bars.

32. Pygmies

Gristle and I sprung a surprise launching party Thursday night, but hardly any one showed up. Some surprise.

For a slew of days now, we've been busying ourselves stitching 'n gluing together two wood kayaks, Arctic Terns by name. Sort of like building a ship in a bottle, only these boats came in cardboard boxes. Both craft were conceived by Pygmy Boats in Port Townsend, Washington, and birthed in my San Rafael, California, garage. The whole labor lasted about three weeks, which at first seems a mite long, but when you figure in the size of the assembled tikes, it's actually just about right (though I'm certainly glad it didn't last any longer).

This Thursday was to be a celebration of our maiden voyage, but—besides Gristle and me—only Sam came out to party at San Quentin Beach. Maybe we should've told everyone, rather than keeping the fete a surprise. Traditionally, a boat is baptized in a flowing river of champagne before a cheering crowd, but that didn't happen this Thursday evening. Not only did the crowd fail to materialize, but Gristle forgot the champagne, left it in the frig at his house.

If the rare truth be told, THE reason to have a launching party is so all your buds can whomp you on the back and offer congratulations on producing such a fine looking craft. It's an ego thing, but when you've been in labor for three weeks, it's hard to get enough strokes. Fortunately for us, a stranger walking his leashed Border Collie along the cliff above the beach oooed-and-awed over the boats when we sauntered by. That was good for a tingle up the ego. Down on the beach, a swimmer came ashore and peppered us with praise, which didn't hurt, either.

Praise for something I've built, I must admit, is as frequent as the raising of the Titanic. I try, I really do, but where other folks have opposable thumbs, mine just seem to be in opposition. Some may produce objets d' art, I create objets d' fiasco. It's a fact. Fortunately for this project, Gristle worked elbow-to-elbow with me on his own boat while I fretted over mine.

Gristle, when he's not paddling, is an artist, a metal sculptor to be specific. His thumbs manage quite nicely, not only with steel and the like, but with just about any medium they brush up against. That includes thin sheets of quarter-inch-thick African mahogany and fiberglass, the patented DNA of our Arctic Terns.

No telling how the boat would've turned out had I been working alone. At one point, Gristle taps me on the shoulder while I'm wiring one side of the kayak to the hull and asks, "Whatya' up do?"

"I'm wiring one side of the kayak to the hull," I say.

"That's right," he says, "but you're stitching the bow of the side to the stern of the hull."

"Oh, yeah, I see," I say, not really seeing. But I pull out the wire stitches and realign the long strips of Serengeti-colored plywood the way they're sketched in the construction manual, which I should read, but never do. That's pretty much the way the whole project goes. Gristle poking, prodding, and jimmying back into place sections of boat I've shanghaied into distortions and juxtapositions.

But I did have my moments, the most notable happening late one evening. Working alone, I've just sanded down a glue line beading up out of the joint where four pieces of desert-swirled plywood come together to fashion the stern. Carrying the smoothed deck into the garage, I angle around a tight corner a bit too sharply and knock a long inch off the stern's sharp end. That's the downside. The upside is I found some old white carpenter's glue and fused the broken tip back onto the boat with hardly a fracture line showing. Barely noticeable, unless you know it's there.

Despite my all-thumbs approach to disfigurement, the magic in the boat's lines and curves appears like an eager rabbit out of a classy top hat. Where two flat strips of plywood lay side by side on the garage floor, after they've been stitched together with pieces of 3" wire, a section of previously uninspired hull mysteriously curves into a rounded chine, then plummets into a hypnotic keel line. It was Origami, but instead of folding flat sheets of paper into flapping cranes, you conjure sheets of plywood into floating kayaks.

In our compleat boats, the three of us paddle out of San Quentin without an inkling of where we're heading. I sight down the Richmond-San Rafael Bridge toward Point Richmond. About a mile out, a large barge with a huge dredging crane snuggles up close to the silver-gray span.

"Wanna head over there?"

"Sure."

"OK, now that we're here, where'dya wanna go?"

"How about over to Chard Island?"

The tide's flooding, but it's early on and our normal landing is littered with a tumble of exposed, two-tone rocks, tops green with marine vegetation and bottoms besotted with dark mud stains. We amble around to the narrower west side of the island and find a flush of beach just wide enough for three kayaks. Pictures of the new boats are snapped, food and beverages consumed.

"Where to now?"

"Let's go back to the prison."

The water's a bit choppy, but not enough to wet your coaming, and the crossing's a breeze. The boat fits like a slipper—pointy toe and all—and is easy to maneuver: simply nudging thighs this way or that against hip braces scoots the kayak in the right direction. At 14 feet long (just this side of short for an ocean-going kayak), the boat handles the water's chop like my college-day's MGA handled bumps in the road—you feel em, but they don't get in the way.

Peaked bows and handling aside, perhaps the boat's strongest feature for aging paddlers—at least on land—is it's heft. A copper farthing under 30 pounds, hiking it up the cliff from San Quentin Beach is an effortless affair. It's a shame no one else is around to witness our kayak toting prowess.

Maybe we'll tease more paddlers out next week. The champagne should be real cold by then.

Stats

Distance: Out to the horizon and back.
Speed: Comfortable.

Time: A couple hours.

Spray factor: Mild.

Dessert: A whole white chocolate chip cookie and part of a carob one Sam couldn't finish at the Fourth Street Farmer's Market after the paddle.

PS For a photo and marketing chitchat on the new boats, check out this commercial site:

http://www.pygmyboats.com/arctic%20tern%2014.htm

33. Gepetto's Whale

Come up with a flashy lure—"party" and "champagne" are pretty flashy—and they'll dredge a channel to your dock.

The square of last week's three paddlers showed up Thursday evening. All in all, nine guys materialized at Sausalito's Schoonmaker Cove to help us christen our new handmade boats. Besides Gristle and me, there were Jay, Wild Bill, Sam, Truckee Steve, Adam's Dad, Cycling Tom (an old pedaling partner of mine), and Indiana.

His new boat also among the unchristened, Indiana reverently added a bottle of champagne to the three Gristle and I ponied up. We emptied one magnum on the three boats, then polished off another ourselves to sanctify the solemn occasion. The remaining two we stowed for after the paddle.

Eileen, Jay's first mate, sculls most mornings. The past couple weeks, she's consistently spotted whales in a little Bermuda Triangle between Knox Point on Angel Island, Peninsula Point on Belvedere, and the water treatment plant in Sausalito. This morning, she sighted a large critter midway between Knox Point and the treatment plant. Filled with the spirit of the evening, we headed in that direction after clearing the cove into Richardson Bay.

At first, the waters were calm with just a whiff of a breeze. But as we paddled south, the two got into a tug of war with each other, the wind playing cat to the water's mouse. Nothing serious, mind you, just a bit of jostling here, scampering there. I was a bit concerned for Cycling Tom—this was his first time in a sit-in—and suggested we head toward shore and the treatment plant where the elements were better behaved.

A loud holler from shore, Sam bellows out, "Thar she blows!"

A water spout 50 yards from the treatment plant scoots high into the air. Then another, and still another. Long bursts and short ones repeat over and over. Could've been Morse Code sounding a dive . . . cause after one particularly lengthy blast, the whale's long, barnacled body slowly arches through the water, flukes pointing skyward, then sinks below the surface.

When we arrive at the dive site several minutes later, the creature still hasn't surfaced. We sit in our kayaks a minute or so before a large, dark form breaks the water's surface 20 or 30 yards to the south of us. From where we sit, this whale feels bigger than before, a real Gepetto's Monstro. It shoots repeated plumes of water skyward before sliding under the surface again, its giant flukes-- bigger than my 14-foot-long kayak—setting up swirling eddies in the water where they pass through.

This time round, the big mammal is down two minutes before it comes up for a breather. Back on the surface, it continues to entertain us with its fancy water works. The show is better than the Cirque du Soleil, though I doubt three rings would be fitting enough for such a grand attraction. Lacking the remains of a Captain Ahab shackled to its side and moving at the lazy speed of a Barcalounger, the big gray is way more entertaining than the frightening it could be. At least I don't feel uncomfortable in its presence. . . until Sam starts his ramblings.

"Didya know that gray whales are one of the few sea creatures that'll chase you down if it feels threatened?"

"Really?"

"Yeah, that's why whalers would leave the big ships and try to harpoon the animal from smaller boats. Most figured it was better to gamble the lives of a few men than have the gray ram and sink the whole road show."

"You don't say."

"Oh yeah, grays can be really fierce. I suppose that's what makes 'em so noble, what captures our attention. Have you seen the post office's new whale stamp?"

"Uh uh. What's the whale doing?"

"Flipping a boatload of five whalers into the air with it's tail."

"Uh huh."

Now I'm beginning to feel uneasy. The image I see on my new stamp is a grinning whale with a bent wood kayak stuck in its maw like a toothpick. The next time Monstro sounds, I suggest we head back . . . only because it's getting late, nothing more. Maybe the others are floundering in the same thoughts I am because there's hardly a flare of dissention.

When we reach Schoonmaker, we're still high on whale-sparked adrenaline and opt to paddle to Strawberry Point on the opposite end of Richardson Bay rather than call it an evening. Half way there, Jay tosses a random glance back towards San Francisco's fading skyline. His jaw drops, and he points straight armed at a distant high-rise gleaming in the Embarcadero Center. A giant "7" is emblazoned on the building's glass side. It's a whale of a "7" and hard to miss. The tail's probably 20 stories tall and the top a block wide.

The last of the sun's reflecting rays are trying to tell us something important. A cosmic sign of stellar proportions. A message from the stars.

But we can't figure it out and make a mad dash for the beach at Schoonmaker and the last two bottles of champagne.

Stats

Distance: Eight miles.
Speed: Sometimes fast, sometimes slow.
Time: Three hours.
Spray factor: Miniscule.
Dessert: The last two slices each of peach and blackberry pies with a chocolate chip cookie chaser.

34. Split Pea Soup

The Goddesses rolled in Monday all hot and steamy. They put a pressure cooker over the entire Bay Area, making everyone scratchy hot and uncomfortable. The smoldering bay waters looked like they'd been flattened under a steamroller, the gals were that heavy-handed. And not a sea breeze to put out the fire.

The air was still thick with Goddess glow when we met at 5:30 PM at Corte Madera Creek. Of the seven paddlers, Gristle was best prepared for the heat: his hand-woven Panama hat—doused in the salty bay—acted like a swamp cooler, the air kicked up by his forward progress squeezing through the loose, wet weave to cool his pate. DA Chris, Wild Bill's nephew, faired almost as well as Gristle: he paddled a sit-on-top and exposed his entire body to whatever spray his blades could dredge up. The rest of us—Sam, Wild Bill, Now 'n Again Ben, Indiana, and I—could do no better than immodestly hike up our spray skirts to let the heat escape from our boats' swampy interiors.

Midway down the channel toward San Pablo Bay, the lid unexpectedly blew off the cooker, and the high pressure's escape whipped up a breeze that stirred the waters and broke the temperature's back. It all happened in a matter of seconds, between paddle strokes. I'd never had a close encounter with a high pressure zone breaking up like that and was surprised to discover that it was a very solid, concrete moment, no less substantial than a slap on the face or a pinch on the tush.

In the swelter of seven boats nosing out the channel, three were hand-built wood vessels: two of them Gristle's handiwork and one mine. Most of the tools we used to construct our craft were hand- rather than grid-powered, which is a good thing if you live in the once great state of California. As the current energy gouge deconstructs the state into developing country status, hand tools soon may be the only ones that work. And with gas prices levitating (if you look closely, you can see the strings), kayaks may become the water transport of choice.

Cruising back to the future across San Pablo Bay in our off-the-grid vessels, we stumbled across a channel opening just this side of Paradise that none of us had encountered before. Because the north bay is shallow and filled with silt, the water here is usually a murky brown hue with occasional overtones of gullshit gray (though a sunset reflecting off the surface can change that to spectacular golds, oranges, ochres, and reds). The further we went into the unknown channel, however, the more the water looked like split-pea soup, in both color and texture.

Lining the banks of the suspect brew were millings of mallard ducks, usually four or five males jealously surrounding a single female. Though the ducks were Jurassic in stature (something in the water?), it was evident that the big males didn't carry much weight with the females, the latter waddling this way and that to escape the attentions of the former.

The only time the females expressed any interest in a male was when Sam cruised by. The sight of him paddling his long, yellow-decked kayak drove them into a frenzy, and they'd plop into the pea soup and swim after him. The males would quack fiercely, but not a female looked back. At one time, six or seven of the crazed females were closing in on Sam's stern. He was barely able to stay ahead.

It was only Sam the females were interested in. They paid no attention to the rest of us. Ignored us, actually. Perhaps in an unconscious effort to catch the attention of the feathered beauties, several of us sprinted past and continued on down the channel at a gallop.

After a while, the channel began to zig and zag, left and right. The ducks were far behind now, but we continued our mad pace, anyway. At one particularly tight corner marked by a round, creosoted post, I pushed my new, untried boat to the limit and leaned as far as I could to make the sharp turn around the marker at speed. The kayak tipped up on its side, the cockpit's edge submerged in the green, syrupy water. For a moment, I envisioned triumphantly brushing my keel high up along the post as I sped by.

It only took Indiana a few minutes to fish me out of the thick, pepper green goo and help empty my boat of sludge. The kayak recovered quite nicely, but my clothes looked and smelled like hand-me-downs from the Creature in the Black Lagoon. Their subhuman condition prompted me to do a laundry the next morning, which inspired me to scrub the bathrooms, which led to a vacuuming of the entire house and a major cleanup of the patio.

I think it was the water made me do it. Some mind-altering contaminant we should alert the EPA to. Sandy says maybe, but—whatever it was—it couldn't be that bad and that I should go back and paddle there again. Soon.

Stats

Distance: About as far as an excited duck can swim.
Speed: Too fast.
Time: Couple hours.
Spray factor: On and off.
Dessert: Cactus Berries at Joe's.

35. New Guy

Besides Gristle, Sam, Jay, Wild Bill, Truckee Steve, Indiana, and myself, a new paddler joined the group Thursday evening: Rick, a friend of Adam's dad, showed up at San Quentin Beach sporting a sleek surf ski. A wild guess between 30 and 50 (kayakers all look alike in that age group), he handled his long, narrow ski with confidence and aplomb. Which really irked us older paddlers to no end.

When Indiana signed on months ago, he showed the same flare for paddling a ski, but he, at least, had the social grace to fall off the beast on a more or less frequent basis. Rick, on the other hand, had the temerity to stay on board in some rather testy waters Thursday evening.

When we left San Quentin around 6:00 PM, a mild breeze was rubbing up against our hulls like a cat looking for affection. Half way across the bay to Tiburon, those little cats-paws turned into meaty claws and really slapped the sides of our boats around. Jostled the waters pretty well, too. Skis are temperamental, sensitive critters and are easily upset by rough treatment. In conditions like we were in (gusty, following seas), they'll frequently roll over on their backs and play the passive, submissive animal, begging for mercy.

We waited for Rick's mount to buckle under the pressure, but it never did. Kept right on going, upright and sprinting past those wind-whipped waves. Wasn't any better when we turned around and paddled back, head first into the 25-knot gusts: in fact, I'd say the boat's performance was even more disappointing. His kayak either jumped over or plowed through the cresting tops without showing the slightest concern for the unruly conditions or the delicate egos sloshing around him.

Not a very auspicious first paddle, but I'm sure Rick'll find the social wherewithal to do better next time.

Speaking of next time, has anyone out there seen Albert? I have it on shallow authority (heard it through the fishnet) that he has very little time to paddle now that he's kayaking so much. A truly sad state of affairs.

Also through the fishnet—and a topic of discussion during our mid-transit raft-up—was news that Red Rock, a stub of an island just south of the Richmond-San Rafael Bridge close to Pt. Richmond, was for sale. For a paltry $10 million US, the sound of rush-hour traffic, passing ferries, cigarette boats, tugs, freighters, oil tankers, and angry seagulls can be yours. Access, though, is pretty much limited to kayaks and row boats. Less than a mile from Pt. Richmond, it'd be a decent swim, too, though keeping your grocery bags dry in crossing could be bothersome. (For pics, history, and other Red Rock tidbits, check out this site: http://www.redrockisland.com/).

The freeboard on my Arctic Tern was more grist for the speculation mill during our mid-course snack. Freeboard is the distance between the water line and the deck of a ship, and more than one of our mishap of eight wondered at the difference in freeboard between Gristle's boat and mine (both kayaks are identical and were floating side-by-side in the raft-up). "Why," they asked, "does your boat sit deeper in the water than Gristle's?"

Wild Bill thought it had something to do with excess ballast in my cockpit. To test his unorthodox theory, he offered me a box of little wispy lemon-flavored cookies. Having an appetite for things scientific, I agreed to his unspoken experiment and ingested a carefully measured slew of the sugary treats right there and then. The amount of freeboard showing on my Tern did not change, not in the slightest. So, though it was an interesting hypothesis—and the cookies were good—Wild Bill's idea clearly doesn't hold water.

(Personally, I don't think we'll ever fathom the mystery of my missing freeboard. In a world of inexplicable phenomena, this one ranks right up there with the Mystery Spot in Santa Cruz, California, and two-headed snakes.)

While we bobbed in the bay conducting weighty experiments, the winds did a nose dive and all but disappeared. Their absence left us with a remarkably balmy evening, the stuff of tropical isles. With the wind and surly seas gone, our group's energy level relaxed to a pace just above a detectable heart beat. Except for catching and surfing the combined wake of two passing ferries in the channel, our return to San Quentin Beach slipped by without noteworthy incident.

No, no, I'm wrong about that. In all the times we've paddled past the prison's spindly lookout towers, the guards have rarely chatted with us. This evening, as we drifted by the East Tower just after sunset, we spotted the dark silhouette of a guard—framed against a sleepy pastel-blue sky and outlined in the orange crime-deterring glow of prison-yard spotlights—on the open platform next to his lookout.

"Pretty nice evening, huh?"
"Yeah, sure is nice. Much better now that it's cooled off."
"Gets pretty hot up in that tower, does it?"
"Some days in the summer, you think you're gonna fry."
"Sounds real hot."
"It is."
"Well, take care."
"You, too."
What more can I say.

Stats

Distance: Seven miles.
Speed: A little over two knots.
Time: Close to three hours.
Spray factor: Frisky at times.
Dessert: Wild Bill could've brought a bigger box of those little lemon-flavored cookies (for purposes of scientific inquiry).

36. Bricks

"Jeez, wouldya looka what the catfish just drug in."
"Hey, it's Albert!"
"Whereya been, Albert?"

His answer is a long one, conjuring up deep channel crossings, mystical isles in fog-shrouded seas, overnights on hidden beaches . . . really, "I've been kayaking so much," he hasn't had time to paddle, he sheepishly explains. With us, anyway.

Alongside Albert are two new faces: Sheila and her first mate, Peter. Both have stretched out long, slender surf skis at the water's edge. Sheila's ski is easily recognizable as a Futura, primarily because the name is emblazoned across the hull in bold letters. Peter's plain white boat is more of an enigma, a regular tabula rasa with no identifying marks of any kind.

Uncluttered by the hieroglyphics of mercantile culture, the boat's character can only be guessed at. Watching our eyes ponder the extreme V-shaped hull, the deep cockpit in an anorexic 18"-wide beam, and a rocker from Whistler's Mother's chair, Peter speaks for the ski.

"A great boat," he says. "That long keel gives it great stability, plus you're even more secure 'cause you're sitting so low in the hull. And that wicked rocker make's turning a dream. A better handling boat you won't find anywhere."

Albert's eyes are big as life preserver rings. "Can I try it?" he pleads.

"Sure," answers Peter, a subtle grin touching his eyes as Albert turns his back to push the skinny boat off the sand into the water.

A duckling learning to walk—that's the imagine that comes to mind watching Albert struggle with Peter's boat, whose true character quickly emerges from behind its pallid face. A lot of stumbling, lurching, and hesitation mark Albert's progress, but to give him credit, he only falls off twice, and those in quick succession.

His finicky boat back on the beach, Peter turns to me and asks if I'd like to try it.

"Ha!" in no uncertain terms.

Gristle and his buddy Jack are on the beach, too, but not paying much attention to Albert's antics. This is their shakedown cruise before heading off for the Green River in Utah and a two-week paddle. They're busy arranging their boats. Jack should be launching a new 17-foot Arctic Tern he's just finished building for the trip, but the last coat of resin is still tacky, so he's paddling Gristle's 14-foot Tern.

Gristle himself is busy stuffing bags of bricks into his bow and stern. There are a lot of bags. One hundred pounds worth. "I gotta know how this boat handles with a heavy load before I get out on that river," he explains.

A hundred pounds is a mess of bricks (some broken, most whole), and it takes Gristle an inordinately long time to arrange them in his boat. In the meantime, the rest of us have taken to the sea, anxious to see what the Goddesses will offer up. Under warm skies, the water's are slow and flatfooted leaving Schoonmaker, but further out, they rev up into an Irish gig, the wind teasing them into some pretty fancy footwork. Peter's skittish boat obviously is not content with the rest of the group's slower two-step, so it takes off on it's own high-spirited, solo dance around Angel Island.

That leaves nine of us (Albert, Sheila, Jay, Sam, Adam's dad, Indiana, and me) once Jack and Gristle catch up. We head over to the water treatment plant in hopes the whale who's been hanging in the bay will be there, but to no avail. The gray has more than likely split for the warmer and more laid-back Latino beat of Baja waters.

I suggest we samba across the bay to Angel Island. The Goddesses, meanwhile, have upped the tempo, and both wind and sea have kicked their dancing into a more frenzied cadence, the Twist or maybe the Mashed Potato. Some in the group hesitate at the crossing, only because Jack, a fairly novice paddler, is in an unfamiliar boat and may not be comfortable with the conditions. Jack, however, is fine with the idea, and we proceed.

Now, you've got to understand that—over the past couple years—our little mishap of paddlers has pretty much been all guys. Call it the curse of the Goddesses, but that's just the way it's been. Had Sheila not been with us this evening and had Jack gone over (which he did not), this is how it might have played out:

"Hey, look, Jack just fell in."

"Yeah, but the wind and current'll blow him right into Angel Island."

"Far out! He can catch the 6 o'clock ferry if he hurries."

"Cool. Let's raft up and eat something."

Sitting on her open-faced ski in those tippy waters, Sheila never lets Jack out of her sight. Even asks him, now and again, how he's faring. Strangest behavior, because after a while, the rest of us begin to take notice of Jack and paddle a little closer, too. Even strike up some idle banter with him. Very strange behavior for us, indeed, like we've downed a six-pack of Luna Bars and picked up an extra X chromosome, which I guess we have for the evening.

Though it isn't a six pack or loaded with X chromosomes, Sam does haul out of his chilled cockpit two bottles of exquisite beer—one light, one dark—at raft-up. It must've been the aromatic sound of those bottle caps popping off, because Peter magically reappears at that very moment from his circumnavigation of Angel Island. To celebrate his rite of passage, Jack hefts a large thermos of homemade margarita slushies from his dry bag, which complement very nicely the peach pie Adam's dad divvies up among us.

To cap off a fine evening, Albert later pays tribute to the old adage, "What goes around, comes around," by pulling off two flawless Eskimo rolls in Schoonmaker Cove. Very slick, but not good enough to erase that earlier tumble off Peter's ski. It'll take at least three consecutive rolls to forget that one, Albert.

Stats

Distance: Not too far.
Speed: Inconsequential.
Time: Well spent.
Spray factor: Decent.
Dessert: Added several more wedges of peach pie to our digestive tracts later in the evening at the Startaj in Sausalito.

37. Brownout

This evening was a stellar confluence of astronomical and secular events. On the galactic level, it was the summer solstice. On a more local level (confined to the planet earth), it was the first of several impromptu people-powered brownouts.

The Goddesses masterminded the summer solstice to highlight the civilizing attributes of sipping cactus berries into the wee hours among like-minded nature lovers. The Ladies, however, had little to do with the brownout, which was a human-inspired event marking an intraspecies disagreement over control of the world's light switches.

(Footnote: As a literal pledge of support for the brownouters, I'm foregoing use of the questionable letter "Y" and the hurtful word "gouge" in tonight's paddle report. Serious omissions, but someone's got to make them.)

Given the auspicious nature of the evening's combined celestial-secular events, we invited our families along. Sandra joined me, and Cathie, Indiana's spouse, accompanied him. Indiana also brought along Katie, the eldest of his three daughters, and her doting male escort, J.P. Now-n-Again Ben's wife, Svetlana, joined us after the paddle as did Eileen and her mate. Sam and Albert did the bachelor thing.

Indiana, the embodiment of the midwestern gentleman, bought an inflatable, two-person boat for his wife and daughter to paddle. The vessel, though large and stable, was about as effortless to coax through the water as a beached whale. Adding insult to strained shoulders and wrists, the boat's paddles had the heft of steel crowbars with lead weights welded on either end.

Though Indiana shared his own fast, lightweight boat and paddle with other fast, lightweight vessels during the evening's course, I never saw him in the rubber beast. Not once. No doubt, there's a reasonable explanation for this most unmidwestern-like behavior, but I can't imagine what it is.

As for me, I outfitted Sandra in the effortless-to-paddle Arctic Tern I had just stitched and glued together. It was her first time both in a sit-in and a rudderless boat, and she did quite well, paddling up- and downwind without misadventure. A few nautical miles under her hull, she asked to switch to a sit-on-top to compare the two boats. After ten minutes of paddling our open-decked Tupperware special, she shouts over to me, "I like the sit-in better, it goes a lot faster with less work." This, of course, was the right thing to utter.

Though we just diddled along the waterfront near Schoonmaker Cove for a couple hours, appetites were soaring at paddle's end. The boats cartopped, we claimed a quadrant of sand on the deserted beach and spread out four blankets to feast on.

What a mishap of diet-challenged hippies we were: salads—green lettuce, red potato, twisted pasta, diced fruit, and mushed vegetable—and little else filled the designer bowls we set out. Albert, a single sharp dogtooth short of boomer weirdness, saved the picnic with two bar-b-cued chickens in plain plastic wrap.

For the next two hours—until 10 PM and the end of the brownout—we ate and drank under an ink-black heaven, our sole light struggling from two faint-hearted candles Eileen and her mate had lit. Though I can't recall all we discussed, I do remember voices becoming quite subdued when none of us sugar-loving hippies could muster up dessert.

Albert—a living, breathing incarnation of the Scout's "Be Prepared"—came to our rescue again, conjuring up a multitude of little jellied beans packed in a clear jar the size of a container ship. With this generous sleight of hand, our solstice brownout came to a sweet end.

Stats

Distance: To the end of the brownout.
Speed: Discreet.
Time: Carefree.
Splatter factor: Civil.
Dessert: Albert's jellied beans.

38. Poison Oak

"Hey, I know you," says Albert to Danny as they offload boats. Danny looks skeptical; the last time he paddled with us, Albert hadn't yet joined the group.

"You know me, but I don't recognize you."

"Sure," says Albert, "we used to play squash together at Berkeley."

"When was this?" asks Danny, who, like the rest of us senior paddlers, probably hasn't been able to create new memories in the last dozen years, let alone keep track of old ones.

" 'Bout ten years ago, I think," says a younger Albert.

"We were friends?"

"Sure, we got along."

And on that reassuring note, their old/new friendship picks up en rapport.

Besides Danny and Albert, four others show up at Gristle's secret launch this side of Paradise—Jay, Indiana, Sam, and me. Though it's close to Paradise, you won't find any old Granny Smiths tempting you here. Nope, not an ounce of original sin, unless you consider the consequences of urushiol—the bitter juice of poison oak—worse than original sin. Towering forests of the plants stand guard over the launch site.

"We gotta go through that," worries Albert, gesturing to the wall of shiny green and red leaves that hide the bay's blue waters.

"Only reason this place is so pristine, Albert, is cause that rash of growth keeps out all the sinners."

Albert remains an unbeliever, but we coax him through the glistening jungle to the little cove. The bashful water's an hour shy of high tide and hides any bottom mud that might otherwise discourage a righteous launch. Albert still has the doubting look of a gavur in his eyes, but once he's afloat, that all changes and he's a believer again.

Hard not to be a believer this evening. The Goddesses have really out-done themselves: Havana warm, mild Aegean currents, Easter Island breezes, and Tongan swells. And that compared to the last three days of Leningrad cold, Tierre del Fuego rips, Nebraska winds, and Jackie Chan chop.

We paddle and surf mild, wind-driven waves in following seas four miles around Tiburon peninsula to Paradise Park (not to be confused with our secret launch). On a narrow stretch of "fee use only" beach (we look for but can't find the feemeister), we prop up our sagging energy with several silver-wrapped Clif Bars and swill it all down in a yeasty microbrew Jay and Indiana have packed in.

Content, we stand out of Paradise Park to Raccoon Straits. In route, we pass the old sub base that guarded this end of the bay during WWII. Rusted orange and black remnants of a heavy chain fence the navy strung under water to ensnarl enemy subs lie in tumbles on the muddy shore. A small fish hatchery aside, the base is deserted, it's acres of chipped and worn concrete empty of activity.

An easy paddle from the base is Pt. Bluff, a projection of uneven rock that marks the northeast corner of Raccoon Straits. When California's great Corcoran lake—its fresh waters covered most of the Central Valley—burst through the Carquinis Strait 560,000 years ago, the brown flood gouged deep channels into what later became the bay. Raccoon Straits boasts a 160-foot-deep slash, second only to the Golden Gate's 313 footer.

Water coursing around Pt. Bluff into the deep strait is often confused and mean-spirited. Back eddies, rips, whirlpools, and counter currents aren't unusual. What's unusual this evening is the absence of any of the above. It isn't any rougher than what I imagine Lake Corcoran might have been like on a calm Pleistocene day.

We continue around the bluff in ideal conditions towards Sam's Anchor Café, a trendy waterfront hangout in Tiburon. Midway between the bluff and the café, a young lady and her two male escorts appear on the third-floor balcony of one of many large, glass-fronted cliff homes gracing the Raccoon's Tiburon side.

"Weeeooouuu!" she screams down to us, gesturing at our boats.

"Weeooouuu!" we holler back up to her.

"Hey, I'll throw a beer down to you guys," and she disappears into her glass house. The potential outcomes of her kindness are quickly apparent: either her aim is off, the bottle of beer hits the water far from us, and sinks; or, her aim is dead-on, she clobbers a boat, and it sinks. Before the young lass reappears on the balcony, we're speeding round the bend of Tiburon Harbor for the safety of Sam's.

Sam's may not be all that safe, though. One Saturday evening two years ago, Jay and I paddled into the restaurant from an Angel Island camp out (in search of food and beer). The place was a sardine can of activity, expensive cruisers and yachts queuing up in the harbor to get a berth. We wiggled our way onto the dock and were inching toward the food when fisticuffs broke out in front of us between a robust Blonde and a willowy Redhead. As we were sidling around the snarling combatants, the Redhead grabbed the Blonde's long, silky hair and flung her sideways into a nearby boat. A few punches later, the police arrived and justice was served.

No such luck this evening . . . no police, no brawls, no crowds, and, we discover, little money in our dry bags for food or drink. Reluctantly, we retrace our strokes, 7-miles worth of them, back to the secret launch, now a secret take-out. It's close to 10 PM and very dark, no lights along this reedy shore. Fortunately, Jay homes in on the secret spot like a pigeon to statuary, and we lug the boats to our cars, thankful we can't see the poison oak. According to a philosophy prof I had in school, the plants may not be there at all for the very reason that we can't see them. Unfortunately, they are there and here's a good web site to help clear up that misconception: http://poisonivy.aesir.com/

Stats

Distance: Fourteen miles.
Speed: Depends on what's tumbling your way.
Time: Three point seven-five hours.
Spray factor: Timid.
Dessert: One luscious tangerine sunset.

39. Paddlette Report

Two disparate events come together here...both having to do with water. Be patient.

On July 4, the intrepid Animal, his mate Punque (me), Wild Bill and Bella Claudia disembarked from Buck's Landing --not fast enough to miss a cheerfully drunk, pot-bellied patron lighting an explosive device the size of a small Ford pick-up. It missed us.

Up Gallinas Creek we paddled. The sky was alight with every rosy and pale blue color on the Goddesses' palette. The contrast with the dark waters and marsh grasses was almost unbearably pretty. Warm air and the occasional duck taking off suddenly and gracefully from the marsh grasses within feet of us completed the picture.

And then the moon rose. The Animal, who was dutifully paddling at 10% capacity to match my 110%, remarked that it felt like a Disneyland Ride where fake alligators or pirates would suddenly appear. Not a comforting thought when one's stability is already gravely in question. Don't get me wrong, I love the Arctic Tern, heroically built by my mate (under the expert eye of Gristle) in the heat of late Spring day after day after day in the driveway. It's just that she and I are working through maiden voyage stuff together--- things like not being sure at first my posterior would actually fit into the seat. Then, the problem of improper alignment of body and boat (oh, there's a back rest?!). And the basic issue of being a sit-in paddled by someone who thinks an Eskimo roll involves cake and ice cream...

The moon coaxed us farther and farther from Olde Buck's, pulling us toward the Marin County Fair whose claim to fame was a toilet art contest. No kidding. At least they used new toilets. As we rounded a bend, we could see the ferris wheel glowing. People were out on their porches in the warm summer air, all waiting for the same thing that we had come to see—the fireworks.

It's probably helpful to know that the ferris wheel lights have to be doused in order for people to be able to actually discern the fireworks. That will explain why the highlight of the evening was the post-fireworks rafting where the Animal and Wild Bill demonstrated how to merge out kayaks into one flotilla. In the middle and stable at last! This was following by the Animal's ritual offering of trail spoor-like sports "cookies", only to graciously acquiesce to provision of Wild Bill and Bella Claudia's truly amazing lemon cookies and Limoncella libation.

Those of you who know the Animal will find this hard to believe, but his mate is somewhat of a teetotaler. Hearing Limoncella, I envisioned a delicious lemonade and swigged down a big gulp. Only to realize that there was fire amidst the fruit.

The trip back took on a surreal glow. With the motivation of being able to change into dry clothes in the middle of a parking lot filled with men in trucks, I sprinted back. Actually, the truth is that I was sure we wouldn't make it until sunrise unless I persisted. So, unbeknownst to the Animal and Wild Bill, who were waxing rhapsodic about the moon, the air temperature, the creekside architecture and the ducks, I was counting out fifty vigorous strokes and then a rest....fifty vigorous strokes and then a rest in steely-eyed determination. My goal was to avoid having to be towed by the Animal, who was eagerly awaiting a chance to practice with his new gear.

About 48 hours later, I could really appreciate how beautiful the night was and how wonderful the company. First I had to believe I actually paddled to the Civic Center and back before dawn broke. Then I could savor the most amazing July 4th of my life....

Now, for water, part II...the Animal's and my youngest son and I were out trying to buy a sofa (while the Animal's away, the family spenders will play). As we came back toward the entrance to 101 near the Village shopping center, we saw a mother duck on the median with at least 10 tiny ducklings huddled near but unable to hop up to join her. We stopped and put on our flashers and so did the behemoth SUV next to us. Without any planning, the SUV driver and I swooped down on the ducklings and carried them (a handful of three each) to the opposite side of the road where there was water leading into the bay. Six being a critical mass of her babies, the mother duck followed uneasily.

The ducklings who weren't scooped up quickly began to make a run for it, scattering in all directions. By then, everyone was stopped and at least six other people of all ages, shapes and sizes emerged from their cars and engaged in a wordless, synchronized round-up of the errant babies. By then the mother had gathered the early arrivals around her and was paddling off in a rafting formation—she was probably wondering where the hideous baby-snatching apparitions had come from and wanting to put in some real distance. The Animal's youngest and two smiling women deposited the last three ducklings gently in the water and when last seen, Mama Duck had slowed her pace to let them catch up.

It had been a three-minute ballet of strangers, perfectly coordinated in an unspoken common goal: let life prevail.

All the more reason to learn what an Eskimo roll really is....

Stats

Distance: A long, long way on July 4; the decisive 20 feet at curbside on July 7.
Speed: Fast for me; glacial for the Animal.
Time: Timeless.
Spray factor: Don't ask—the mother duck got very nervous.
Dessert: Lemon cookies that melt on the tongue once snatched away from the Animal.

40. Fourth of July

Buck's was unusually busy . . . normally the dusty affair wilts into inactivity long before summer sunset. When Wild Bill, his wife Claudia, Sandy, and I put in at 8:30 PM, the old wood docks and dirt parking lot were buzzing. Kids kicking up dust, barbecues smoking, a few earlybird sparklers winking off and on.

Wild Bill took advantage of the last bit of natural light to cast a barbless line into the seamless waters of Gallinas Creek. He'd just returned from a two-weeker in Italy and was sporting a slick, collapsible rod and reel. It wasn't so much his long casts that were impressive, it was the fact he could snap that pole high above his head and still stay upright in his squirrelly kayak.

For the past 18 months, we've been watching a young fellow spruce up a two-story, red cedar A-Frame house nestled on a floating platform in Gallinas Creek. The last time through, we saw him hammering away on a new dock. This evening, he was sitting in a lounge chair on the finished boardwalk, drink in hand, his house (Hansel and Gretel comfortable with leaded windows and carved doors) glowing warm red in the last oblique rays of light, a look of contentment about him.

"It doesn't get any better than this," he tips his glass in our direction. We stop and chat a short while, complimenting him on the work he'd done. Accolades paddle deep, we move on, swirling through the last, long fingers of sunlight nuzzling up against our hulls.

A mile further down the creek, three alligator-green lengths splash into the water. On the backs of the Tupperware beasts are three Huckleberry Finn-aged kids, black paddles thrashing water. The three turn their sit-on-tops in the same direction we're heading and dissolve into the dark ahead of us.

The whacking of their paddles on Gallinas signals the start of the evening's snaps, crackles, and pops. Some are pop-gun far away, others are butt-jolting close, the friendly water softening those heavier percussive assaults on our ancient hulls.

Syncing in with the noise-makers are random bursts of light. Some powder the distant sky in pastels of patriotic red, white, and blue, an occasional dim whooommp reaching us after the last rub of light fades to black. Closer to shore, a quilt of wire-handled fireflies dodges and darts along the shore. Nearby, the railing of a concrete bridge blazes with a thick line of sparklers and little kids' excited cries.

The number of boats—motor- and human-powered—reaches gunwale-rubbing numbers as we round a bend in the channel. The boats, however, aren't the main attraction: to the west, down a narrow tributary, blinks a gigantic, rotating eye . Shards of primary colors shoot out from a black iris toward the eye's horizon; some of these shards ignite into concentric rings of color that migrate both back to the iris and outward to the horizon's fringes.

The four of us raft up in the crowded waters for a better sightline on the throbbing eye. While we swing our mated boats around, the reason for our late-night outing whines into the sky—first a single red rocket, then a green one, then yellow, white, blue, and a slough of colors I can't name take to the air behind the spinning Ferris wheel.

Marin's Fourth of July fireworks at the county fairgrounds normally isn't an event to write home about. The danger of grass fires keeps the bombs bursting low in the sky and reams of red tape ensnare the size and length of the celebration. Despite these self-imposed caps, the spectacle takes on big-town dimensions when tasted from the backwaters of Gallinas Creek. The twenty-minute show morphs into a fuzzy hour and the entire night dome—not just a sliver—lights up.

On our paddle back to Buck's, the Goddesses treat us to another light show: the moon, a rise away from full, weaves a shadowy path though low-hanging Ichabod Crane clouds. Any other night, the light play would've been spooky, but tonight it's pleasantly dramatic.

Adding a touch of his own surreal glow to the moon's delight, Wild Bill launches a red emergency flare from his boat. The Ladies must have seen it because the clouds part, and we kayak the last half mile to Buck's on rippled moonlight.

Stats

Distance: Six miles.
Speed: Two point four knots.
Time: Two point five hours.
Spray factor: Hardly.
Dessert: Raspberry-flavored cookies and a lemon-flavored, high-octane drink Wild Bill and Claudia brought back from their Italy trip.

41. A Testosterone of Paddlers

A scraggle of us meet in front of Buck's before the paddle: Jay and Truckee Steve are there when I show up; Sam, Indiana, and Rick wander over not too long after my first beer clears the bottle. While the six of us chat up the locals under a shade tree next to the front door, Wild Bill, Ben, Gristle, and his last born, Zeke the Younger, materialize.

Missing is Albert, so we hang around sipping cold beer and talking. One of the locals, a Samoan with boulder-sized biceps and a thick south seas accent, has been laying asphalt in Bolinas all week. He mentions eyeballing the surf feeding into the town's lagoon and how sweet it's been.

This bit of gossip goes down better than free beer—we've got a 10-day kayaking expedition planned for Vancouver Island in early August and have Sunday penciled in to practice rescues and surf launching-landings, which we might need in the B.C. Locally, one of the finer places to flounder in the water is at the mouth of Bolinas Lagoon—the waves are macho big way out, but piddle down to cheer-leader cute close to shore. We, of course, will be practicing far from shore.

Nautical time waits for no paddler, so the ten of us—sans Albert—take our leave of the shade tree and sift through the dusty parking lot to the broken dock and chipped concrete launch ramp. A lone paddler is in the middle of the channel practicing rolls.

"Hey, Albert, you know there's more to kayaking than Eskimo Rolls, don'tya?"

"Yeah, what might that be?" he spits out a mouthful of Gallinas Creek.

"Cold beer."

A wordless roll underscores Albert's feelings on the topic, and the rest of us go about putting in. Assembled on the water, the eleven of us are a serious bunch—a regular testosterone of kayakers. Buoyed by numbers, we feel we're a group to be reckoned with.

We convoy west toward the distant freeway. A mile down the channel, we spot a lone rowboat heading towards us with two occupants. Drifting closer, we prepare to board, but the oarsman turns out to be one of the locals we'd been sipping beer with under the shade tree at Buck's. His excitable Dalmatian pup does a jittery two-step when he sees us, rocking their rowboat a bit this way, a little that way.

"How'd you get out here so fast?" we wonder.

"Took off while you guys were talking," he says. "Great evening to be in the water, huh?"

We have to agree, exchange mandatory pleasantries, and move on. The sea's bounty is limitless, though, and a mile down the channel another rowboat, this one newly painted, approaches. In it we see a guy panting at the oars with a young woman keeping watch in the bow. We come up alongside and inform the two that they'll be free to go if they give us beer.

"All I've got is a Pepsi," says the guy nonplussed, "and you can't have it." The girl snorts and says, "Come on, Jordan, let's go."

Gen-Xers.

The storm drain under the freeway marks the bottom sweep of our yo-yo paddle. Down but anxious to rebound, half our testosterone slips into the narrow opening. The walls are just far enough apart to admit the boats single file. Midway down the long, dark passage, the temperature climbs to sauna hot and the splash of paddles is soundlessly ingested by a contagion on the water's surface thicker than split-pea soup.

Easing around an arthritic bend in the tunnel, we see fading daylight at the far end. And—except for the now-visible thick, green crust of noise-suppressing scum holding the water down—that's all there is at tunnel's end. No booty. No adventure. No one to impress with our prowess. Spent, we limp back to the storm drain's mouth, most of us backwards because we can't turn our boats around in the narrow confines.

Two-thirds of the weary way back to our parked cars, we cross a T in the creek: right is Buck's and left is McGinnis Park and the Club Restaurant. The sun's on a downer and skidding behind

Mt. Tam. We've just enough time to scoot over to the restaurant, chug a beer or two, and make our presence felt.

Our boats scattered across McGinnis' three-kayak-long dock, we hike up the ramp toward the restaurant. "How much cash you got, John?" I haven't got a rusty nickel. No one's got any coin, matter of fact. To save face, we do the only sensible thing guys can do at a time like this: we pee in the bushes, then paddle back to Buck's feeling pretty cocky.

Stats

Distance: Half as far as we could've gone.
Speed: Way fast.
Time: Three hours and counting.
Spray factor: Nothing we couldn't handle.
Dessert: Cactus Berries at Joe's served up in fancy new goblets rimmed with green salt.

42. Ballyhoo of Seals

A ballyhoo of curious harbor seals greeted us from the off-shore waters near Angel Island's Kayak Camp Beach. Big eyes bobbing in mild swells, the slick creatures watched us arrive in waves: Jay's friends Brian and Bambi were the first set, followed by John G. (another of Jay's acquaintances), Jay himself, Ben, and me. The last group to land were Wild Bill, Bella Claudia, Albert, Danny, Sam, and Indiana. Lined up in the sand, we were an even baker's dozen less one.

Since early morning, Albert, playing devil's advocate, had been emailing us weather (read that "wind") reports for Angel Island: 10 AM and the wind's already up to 10 knots; 1 PM and we're talking 24 knots; 3 PM and the wind's shifted into overdrive with gusts up to 30 knots. Not good tidings . . . definitely the stuff of cresting waves and jittery nerves.

But the Goddesses looked favorably on us 'cause by our 7:30 PM launch from Schoonmaker, the pesky breezes had abated, and we glided across the mouth of Raccoon Straits toward the beach with only a few gravity waves—remnants of the defunct wind—to contend with. All under the bluest of twilighted skies.

Kayak Camp is a leg cramp away from the beach, up a steep set of worn-out steps to the top of a grassy knoll with a level field. Perfect for pitching a tent and stowing gear. And we had plenty of gear to stow. The overnight was a wet run for our upcoming Vancouver trip, and we'd stuffed our boats with seven-days worth of supplies.

Among the goodies crammed under the stern hatch of my kayak was a plastic bladder filled with six gallons of water for drinking, cooking, a quick shower or two. We really didn't need the liquid (all 49.98 pounds of it) since the Kayak Camp had it's own spigot of water. But for the backache of an authentic wet run . . .

The best I could do was drop the bloated bladder in the middle of the path and look forlorn. Everyone I knew ignored me. Which was ok because I didn't know everyone. Brian was one of the unknowns, but he's a guy, and guys don't carry other guy's water. Not PC, particularly uphill. Fortunately, Bambi (another unknown) took pity on me and offered to help. The bladder's awkward size argued against two people sharing the burden, so I let Bambi carry it up the hill by herself. It was very PC.

Once tents were pitched and gear stowed, food was brought out. No freeze-dried beans this evening, no siree. We're talking salmon, steak, quiche, a grab of tasty hors d'oeuvres, exotic breads, and enough red wine to fill my own bladder. The weathered surface of the camp's single picnic table swayed to overflowing with the tasty treats.

We ate and drank into the wee hours of the night. The first eve of a new moon, our major source of light was a Duraflame log Albert had paddled over. Actually, our major source of light was a sky lit up under its own power (a necessity in California these days). It was truly stunning, standing on that piece of isolated real estate in the middle of San Francisco Bay and marveling at sprays of luminescence from distant places unimaginable.

Waxing poetic under the stars, a splinter of us took an impromptu hike an hour before midnight. Close to our campsite were several old buildings, part of Camp Reynolds, a Union garrison dating back to Civil War days. We circled the buildings in a round-about fashion, hoping to find a way in, but for knot. On a second loop of the shadowy structures, we stumbled across a narrow singletrack that wove a path over a wooded knoll and then down toward Pt. Knox and Richardson Bay.

Midway along this track, an opening in the woods sighted directly on the Golden Gate Bridge. A low, wispy fog fingered both north and south towers, and the entire span glowed an eerie orange-red in reflected light. A few degrees east were the illumined hills of Pacific Heights. Further along the trail, the nighttime silhouette of San Francisco's high-roller district floated into view. Herb Caen may have groused about that cancerous skyline for the last 40 years of his newspaper career, but it was a jaw dropper this evening.

Prey to sensory overload, our little group traipsed back to camp using the faint glow from Albert's distant Duraflame as a signpost. Sleep waylaid me inside my sleeping bag, and I couldn't get up until morning pushed the creature off. A concern for returning winds helped us break camp early and shore up our gear for a return paddle to Schoonmaker Cove.

Water still bloated my bladder. I looked for Bambi, but she had discreetly vanished. Face-to-face with a long, unassisted stumble down the hillside, I did the macho thing—I pulled the stop-cock and let the water flow. It felt very good.

Stats

Distance: Six miles.
Speed: Lackadaisical.
Time: Twelve hours.
Spray factor: Misty.
Dessert: The first or second bottle of red wine.

43. Crissy Field

Albert says to meet in the parking lot at Crissy Field.

I've never launched from Crissy Field. "Which parking lot is that?"

"The one by the yacht harbor. Meet by the new bathroom."

I get it right on the third parking lot. All the lots close to Crissy Field are near yacht harbors. They all come equipped with fancy loos, too. My problem is I can't tell one head from another; if it's inside and flushes, it works for me. Some people are color blind; me, I'm loo-blind.

Even testing the waters in three different parking lots, I still get to Crissy Field before Albert. While I'm waiting, I hike around the grounds soaking in all the slick, official signage. During the last couple years, this stretch of land on the northwest side of San Francisco has seen big changes, and there's a lot to tell.

In1912, the original marsh here was filled to make way for the Panama-Pacific International Exposition. Nine years later, a U.S. Army airfield opened on the exhibition's Grand Prix racetrack; it was named after airman Major Dana Crissy. San Francisco's Presidio, including Crissy Field, was transferred in 1994 from the U.S. Army to the National Park Service. In 1998, the Park Service set about restoring the land to its original look and feel.

Part of that restoration includes a comely little beach butting up against the bay, perfect for launching and landing a kayak. Temptation outweighing patience, I write Albert off and off-load my boat and equipment to the water's edge. Moments before I push off, Albert squeals into the parking lot. Says he was swept up in a flood of traffic on the Bay Bridge and was lucky to arrive when he did.

Under a sky bolstered in lumpy gray, the two of us launch into a choppy bay. We head west for a while, but as we near the north tower of the Golden Gate Bridge, a large flush of contrary eddies starts thumping the water's surface like a frustrated old maid beating a Turkish throw rug.

"I don't wanna have to do any rescues in that water," Albert says. "Let's head back the other way."

"If you get tumbled, I'll pull you out," I almost say, but think better of it. We've been practicing rescues the last couple weeks, and my novice offer to help could easily be interpreted as a threat.

The wind's at our backs now, really bullying the water along. We're going with a flood tide, too, so the wind—blowing with the flow—doesn't whip up any particularly good surfing waves. But we move along quite nicely, nonetheless. A mile or so down the beachfront, we round a breakwater into Aquatic Park. A few swimmers are adding to the chop, but we haven't come to watch swimmers. It's snack time, and there's a fine little hole-in-the-wall eatery here that serves up a tasty bowl of clam chowder.

Before landing in front of the empty concrete amphitheater, I ask, "You got money?"

"No, I thought you had money."

Paddles dragging, we turn stern and hungrily head back to Crissy Field against wind and tide. The spray's doing high-fives, but my cockpit stays dry 'cause I'm sporting a new sprayskirt with a fancy elastic waistband. It's size "L," but hugs like a cinched up corset on a plump diva singing a skinny Carmen. Normally I'm a tenor; in this outfit, I'm a high C away from a soprano. I'd eaten that clam chowder, I could've auditioned for the Vienna Boys Choir.

Albert and I slosh into Crissy just as four kitesurfers are harnessing up. The kites are bright colors—blues, reds, oranges, yellows—and hang in the wind directly overhead while the surfers strap into their boards. Feet locked in, they angle their kites down to catch wind and take off like jet boats. After a minute or so, all we can see are the high-flying colorful kites, the surfers lost in the confused distance.

Before going ashore, Albert practices a few rolls in the windy water, cleaning most of them. I watch nearby. Among our regular paddlers, Albert has the most experience rolling. But some of the others are catching on fast: Wild Bill, Jay, and Indiana have all managed to roll their boats in the last couple weeks. Me, I'm still hanging onto the side of the swimming pool trying to get upright (when there's a swimming pool to hang onto).

Which is one of the reasons I launched from the San Francisco side of the Golden Gate this Wednesday evening. The monthly BASK meeting is at the UCSF Medical Center tonight, and the main speaker, Tsunami Ranger John Lull, is a noted authority on rolls and rescues. I figure maybe I can soak up some of what he says.

I tail Albert as far as the medical center, then lose him when we swing different directions to park. The center—a confusion of buildings designed by the same architect as the Winchester Mystery House—haunts several blocks on either side of Parnassus Avenue. I can't remember the meeting place's address, but I do remember the room number: 301. I go from building to building, checking each and every room 301. 7:45 rolls around, and I still haven't found the meeting, which started over an hour ago. I try one more building. If this isn't it, I'm bailing.

The good news is I find the meeting place (it's in the nicest room numbered 301 in the entire complex, I can tell you that). I also find Albert, Wild Bill, Bella Claudia, Jay, and Now-n-Again Ben, who says the speaker hasn't spoken, yet. The bad news is the keylime pie earlier gracing the snack table is no more. Not a crumb left. I'm a hungry tenor for another day.

Stats

Distance: Five point seven-five nautical miles.
Speed: Two point three knots.
Time: Two point five hours.
Spray factor: In your face.
Dessert: Vanished.

44. Clayoquot Sound

"That looks higher than seven feet to me," the toll booth attendant at Tsawwassen, British Columbia, said and pulled out what looked like a walking stick Shaq O'Neill might have leaned on. If you believed in reading tea leaves, cat entrails, and mud splatters, this was a deciding moment for our long-planned kayaking trip to Tofino, Vancouver.

Holding the measuring stick next to the trailer, the attendant lowered one end to the ground, the bent metal arm at the top closing down on my kayak's inverted hull. The space between hull and measuring arm narrowed quickly; it looked as though our pre-trip calculations had been off, and we'd end up paying double the crossing fees to Nanaimo, not a good omen at all.

We'd planned this trip to Clayoquot (if you tie your tongue around it just right, it should come out sounding like "Klak'•wit") Sound for six months, but had put off doing anything till the eleventh hour. The logistics of transporting six kayaks 1100 miles each way from San Francisco to Tofino on Vancouver Island was one of those "we'll do it laters." At the last possible minute, we purchased a flatbed trailer and built a large storage compartment and kayak rack over the wood bed. Loaded, all our gear filled the compartment and the boats fit perfectly on the makeshift tower.

Transport in place, we logged onto the Internet to make reservations for the crossing from Tsawwassen to Nanaimo on Vancouver Island. Different fares for different vehicle configurations popped up on the screen. One configuration snagged our attention: if the high point of the vehicle/trailer combo was greater than seven feet, the crossing fee doubled to a rather substantial and wallet blistering figure. We measured. And we measured again. Total height for our trailer-boat combination: eight feet. The next day, we worried the trailer down to a passable height for the Tsawwassen - Nanaimo crossing: 6.5 feet.

The attendant's measuring stick touched ground, and it was obvious we'd miscalculated . . . but only by four inches, which left two inches to spare before breaking the seven-foot barrier. "It sure looked higher than seven to me," the attendant shuck her head and waved us onto the ferry, our wallets a little heavier for our efforts and good fortune locked in for the paddle.

Meares Island

Tofino, our launch point on the northern tip of Vancouver's Esowista Peninsula, was a twisty, mountainous two-hour drive from the ferry terminal at Nanaimo. Rain threatened—but never fell—during our Saturday overnight in the small fishing village, part-time tourist mecca. All available campsites filled months before, we spent the evening in a cozy waterfront motel (using up most of the money saved on the ferry crossing). Sunday morning drizzled in, but was a downpour before breakfast ended. August waters in Clayoquot Sound are cold—in the low 50s (Fahrenheit)—and we came outfitted with thick wetsuits, so rain didn't put a damper on the launch.

A rocky beach slid into the water at the foot of our motel. We offloaded the empty boats at water's edge then bloated them up with all the paraphernalia we'd stuffed in the trailer. In no time, we'd morphed our lightweight kayaks into heavyweights with pots, pans, stoves, water filters, tents, sleeping bags, stores of food, gallons of water, dry synthetic clothes . . . all the trappings of a civilized outing.

Launching out of Tofino, we were a ten-minute paddle from Meares Island (which, on our charts, looked like an enlarged heart surrounded by two undersized lungs). The weather channels we picked up on our VHF radios predicted the current storm to last another full day, mellowing out sometime early Tuesday. On Saturday, while scouting around Tofino for kayaking information, we'd met a local guide who singled out a campsite halfway up Lemmens Inlet (a blade of water that comes to within a nautical mile of splitting Meares into two unequal halves) by Sharp Creek. It seemed a safe place to weather the storm.

Sharp Creek

The site at Sharp Creek—tent-sized open spaces in a tight bundle of red cedar just off a grassy shore—was vacant when we floated in around 1 PM. We set up camp in a downpour, tents bordering a common cooking, gathering, clothes-drying area we covered with a large plastic tarp hung from overhanging branches. Stomachs sated with lunch, three of us—Jay, Indiana, and I—opted to explore further up the inlet. The winds had picked up, and the rain, at times, was break-dancing parallel to the water's surface. Except for the lack of steep chop (not enough fetch for it to build up), we could've been paddling on San Francisco Bay.

Campsites in Clayoquot Sound are few and far between because most of the land Cape-Canavirals straight up out of the water, reaches ear-popping heights, then tumbles back into the sound. Level sites like Sharp Creek are at a premium. Completely covered in dense growths of cedar, spruce, hemlock, and fir, the steep coast's high tide line matches up exactly with the lowest branches of shoreline trees, the even green line mimicking the work of a cosmic hairdresser who's inverted a bowl over the land and clipped the flora even with its rim.

Paddling around a rocky point, Indiana and I spied a large blue tarp tangled up under a bowl-cut tree by the water's edge. Rescued from a bleak future of rips and tears, the tarp found new life back at camp, diverting the rain-that-would-not-stop off our two formerly wet tents. The tarp kept the rain at bay, but it had little impact on the mosquitoes that had moved in with us. Little, but persistent, they latched onto any flesh foolishly exposed and drilled deep. We lathered on repellant, but it only made the pesky critters more aggressive. Smoke and fire, we knew, had stopping power, but building a blaze with wet wood almost proved beyond our citified skills. We finally managed the task with the help of a camper's fire stick, piling up damp wood to dry around the small, struggling fire. The wet wood smoked up a storm, and the mosquitoes temporarily cleared out.

High-Flying Kayaks

Though Sharp Creek, swollen with rain water, still raged down the mountain past our tents like eighteen wheelers, Monday dawned without a drizzle. It also dawned without any water in the cove to the south of us. None. Where Lemmens Inlet had been the day before, an intertidal salad of green pickleweed and shore grass mixed with rusty lettuce kelp glistened alongside green-algae-tinted mud. The only access to the deeper waters north of us was an anemic channel meandering from the mouth of Sharp Creek. Tidal differences in Clayoquot Sound are much greater than in San Francisco Bay, and we hadn't been prepared for the speed and extent to which water scoots in and out of the sound.

The lean tide kept us cornered until 11 AM before we could scrape bottom along the skinny channel that ran into the inlet. Eel grass nudging the surface sided with the now flooding tide, and we followed their green stalks to the northern-most reaches of the channel. The water seethed with jellyfish, platter-sized with long, drooping tentacles. Half way up the inlet, we met our first bald eagle, overseeing her domain from a tall, dead fir. A rare sight for us, we hung around, studying Her Majesty through our binoculars and the zoom lens on Jay's camera. The bird seemed nonplussed by our presence and paid us scant attention, keeping her high perch.

She didn't take to the air, but we did. Figuratively, at least. The waters had become so still and mirror smooth, surface reflections took on a photorealistic quality. We floated around white clouds, skimming tops of cedar-covered mountains. Small rock outcroppings became asteroids suspended in space. It seemed as real as any hallucination I've ever had of flying, maybe more so. But it didn't last long, the sensation jostled apart by a flighty breeze that changed the water from mirror to sandpaper.

Floating Cabins

Paddling up the inlet with the wind at our backs, we stumbled across several oyster farms tucked in close to shore, big plastic barrel floats marking their location. Woven together with ropes, the barrels supported lengths of descending cord, each line spotted with growing clusters of white-shelled oysters. Between farms, we passed a handful of cabins built on floating platforms scattered in secluded coves. One water dweller, Vargas Dan (he used to live on Vargas Island he explained) was a timber sculptor. His cabin sat neatly in the middle of his float, wood boats that'd seen better days hugging either side. One recycled ark he used as a workshop, the other he was slowly coaxing into working condition. A small garden grew on a nearby lump of rock.

We exchanged pleasantries and started the trek back to Sharp Cove. A mile from camp, a Zodiac with a 45-hp Mercury outboard growled up next to us. "You fellows know where the hot springs are?" a thirtyish fellow asked. Next to him in the small boat, his wife and young son looked weather-worn and a tad forlorn. "We've been searching since lunch, and we're completely lost."

"It's north of here, on the upper end of Flores Island," Jay, our trip navigator, showed him on the laminated chart strapped to his deck. "But it's a ways away, maybe 12-15 nautical miles."

"Thanks," the Zodiac's skipper said and zoomed off. Five minutes later, we saw him bobbing in the middle of the inlet, his motor dead. We paddled over and Wild Bill, master tinker, got him up and running in less than 10 minutes. We watched as he sped off, his motor, sounding healthy and confident, fading in the distance. Fifteen minutes later, we paddled into our camp on a high tide. Skies were clear and the sun out in force. We gathered up all our wet sleeping bags, tents, and clothes and spread them out on the grass to dry. While our gear steamed, Indiana jumped into his boat and paddled out to the middle of the small cove.

Rolling

In the weeks leading up to our trip, the six of us had immersed ourselves in self and assisted rough water rescues. We'd even taken a shot at Eskimo Rolls, something none of us had succeeded in up to that time. Wild Bill and Jay had managed a few during practice sessions, but were pretty inconsistent and not feeling all that confident in their rolling acumen. Though we never saw him do it, Indiana claimed he'd mastered a sweep roll in his pool.

"You gonna roll for us, Indiana?" we shouted out to him.
"Watch," he said and capsized the boat.

Before we could even think about tossing out a line,
Indiana rolled the kayak rightside up. Flawlessly. Without a hitch.
A big smile on his face.

"Do it again."

He did, over and over, never missing.

"Ok, ok, you can stop, we believe you," more than a touch
of envy in our voices.

Confused Water

Sharp Creek was back to a trickle Tuesday morning, skies
clear. Over dinner the previous evening, we'd decided to try for
Vargas Island via Maurus Channel on the west side of Meares.
With drinking water in short supply, Indiana and Sam filtered water
out of Sharp Creek with a hand pump. While they filtered, we
listened to the weather forecast on the VHFs. Strong winds were
predicted out of the northwest, and a surf advisory was out. Our
plans changed. Instead of swinging around Meares' exposed west
side, we now planned to paddle around the protected east side, up
Fortune Channel to Mosquito Harbor. With another early morning
ebb sucking up all our water, we waited until 1 PM before we could
launch. We paddled against a mild flood back towards Tofino, then
caught the building current sweeping by the fishing village and
down toward Meares' southeast corner. The strong flood carried us
northward around the point and up the island's backside.

Water flowing around an island is a strange creature. We
butted heads with the beast at Dawley Passage, a narrow gate of
water that opens into the wider expanses of Fortune Channel. Up
to Dawley, we had been moving quickly with the current, a true free
ride. At Dawley, the water became more than confused. It was
downright schizophrenic. Water on the south side of the passage
wanted to move north while water on the other side wanted to flow
south. The outcome was a splashy civil war, neither side conceding
to the other. Fortunately, the battlefield was less than an eighth of a
nautical mile wide, and we slipped through without upset.

The most striking feature of Fortune Channel was the long
swath of clear-cut on the Vancouver side. It was as if a galactic
version of Stephan King's Lawnmower Man had run his twisted
blade the entire length of the mountain, taking out a huge path of

old growth temperate rainforest. Replacing red cedar, Sitka Spruce, and Western Hemlock, a wide belt of salal had moved into the razor-cut slope. Where the old growth pyramided upward, the low-lying salal mushroomed out like exploded Jiffy-Pop popcorn containers.

Mosquito Harbor

Mosquito Harbor floated into view just before 5 PM. Alongside a deep-water cove, tides would have little effect on landing or launching. Behind a shoreline midden of clam shells, a trail ran into the woods where we found skeletal remains of an old settlement. One cabin was still habitable, but none of us chose to bed down in it. Frankly, this section of old growth reminded me of "The Blair Witch Project" and sent shivers lurching up and down my spine. Besides, camping on the open grassy shore was a refreshing change from the dark, troglodyte existence we'd led under Sharp Cove's trees.

Before our tent stakes bit ground, Indiana hurried out into the middle of the cove to practice his rolls. This time his kayak was fully loaded and torqued through the water in stop-frame slow motion. He still managed to come up smiling. "You won't believe how easy it is once you get the hang of it," he said. Now, I'm not one to complain, but Indiana's enthusiasm was beginning to wear thin. Rolling may have been easy for him, a young kid in his mid-forties, who I've actually seen touch his toes with minor knee bending. The rest of us, a good decade or more older, rarely see our toes when we look down.

Catering to our Generation XXL bellies, food on this expedition was anything but fat-farm lean. This evening, Jay whipped up servings of couscous, Jaipur vegetables, Kashmir spinach, Bengal lentils, Bombay potatoes, all spiced with mango chutney. The evening before, Sam had prepared his famous spaghetti sauce concocted from fresh, homegrown vegetables, seasoned with hand-picked herbs, and dished over tender pasta bow ties lightly coated with virgin olive oil. The first night out, Indiana had served us inch-thick steaks, beans, and rice ("it'll help you roll").

We ate well and so did the mosquitoes. These skeeters were the cream of the crop, the pick of the litter, the top guns of the blood suckers. Big, fast, and insatiable, they made the insects at Sharp Cove look like bugs in training. Not even a hot, smoking fire could hold them back. That night, glistening in an oily film of Deet, I fell into a troubled sleep listening to their frenzied thuds against my tent flap. "The Blair Witch Project" was a walk in the park compared to Mosquito Harbor.

Milties Beach

It took only one wake-up call to get us moving Wednesday. We broke camp, had our boats fully loaded, and were cruising shortly after 7 AM. The mosquitoes never bothered us on the water, and that's where we planned to stay. We let the ebb in Fortune Channel carry us north to Matlset Narrows. The water was glass smooth in the channel; ahead of me, the watery impressions left by Ben's paddle strokes set up like dinosaur tracks in Badland's mud.

Lining the channel was a flurry of bald eagles, more than we'd seen on the entire trip. But not as many as we were about to confront in Matlset Narrows, where a great bird perched in every other tree top. The reason for their numbers literally jumped out of the water: the narrows was thick with fish. Towards the end of the waterway, we joined a pod of dolphins. The pod was spread out, and we paddled past individuals and small isolated groups for a nautical mile before they disappeared.

Milties Beach on the north side of Vargas Island was our day's destination. To reach it, we had to cross Calmus Passage, three nautical miles west of Matlset Narrows. Calmus is a major arm of Tofino's waterway to the Pacific with its fishing grounds and tourist attractions. It's also a speedway for private and commercial boats. Six yellow-decked speed bumps, we crossed cautiously, always on the lookout for fast-moving boats. Threading our way through the traffic, it took just under an hour to reach Milties, a quarter-mile stretch of beach with fine—almost powdered—white sand. Facing northwest, Milties surrenders spectacular views of Vancouver's Catface Range, distant Flores Island, and the Pacific Ocean. Except for temperate rainforests blanketing the steep mountains, the scene looked like a tropical snapshot from a Mitchner novel. The unending tourist traffic added to the illusion as did the balmy temperature, in the high 70s, low 80s.

After pitching camp, exploring the beach, and giving in to a catnap, Jay and I gunkholed up the coast toward the Pacific to see what there was to see. Except for the tropical touch, the area fit the standard Clayoquot Sound mold: old growth forests sliding down to the water, lower boughs marking the high tide line, pockets of rock-strewn beaches, and high-flying fish. The only changeling was the water. When the afternoon winds perked up around 4:30, there was enough fetch for windwaves to form and grow. Punching bows through cresting peaks was a satisfying sensation, particularly after having paddled three-and-a-half days on placid, lake-like conditions. Surfing back to camp was downright exciting and reminded both of us how much we missed the open ocean.

Surf

Next morning, Thursday, the six of us took off for the high seas. Skirting round Vargas' northwest corner, we paddled into Pacific swells. Slow-moving, 4-6 foot-high rollers—from southern storms that never reached this far north—lumbered underneath us. Maybe it was the up-and-down of the water, maybe it was all the liquid I'd been downing, but my bladder suddenly felt like it was one drip short of bursting.

The first stretch of beach that loomed into sight was being pummeled by good-sized shore break. I crossed my knees in the cockpit and paddled on with the group. The next length of sand was being battered by equally abusive waves. But my cup was at the uncomfortable point of overflowing, and I wasn't about to move on. The six of us lingered outside the breakers a few minutes watching the sets. We'd spent a day practicing surf landings and launchings before the trip, but our practice waves were small sea potatoes compared to these hull snappers.

I waited for a lull, then paddled madly for shore. Indiana, enthusiastic as always, followed. Twenty-five yards out, another set started rolling in. Following just behind the crests and sliding back into their troughs after they spilled over, we inched closer to the beach. Ten yards from shore, a sneaker popped up behind us, broke into a flood of whitewater soup, and spilled over our boats. My hand-eye coordination has been AWOL for years, but the Goddesses were with me, and I braced my skinny Greenland paddle into the confusion and was pushed parallel into the beach without upending. Indiana didn't fare as well; the surge of water caught him off guard, and he flipped over. The water was too shallow to roll, and he had to wet exit.

Hah! I thought, gratefully adding my own fair share of salt water to the high tide line. "Why bother rolling if you can stay upright?" The logic seemed unimpeachable and buoyed my waning pride. Lighter of body and spirit, we both succeeded in doing a one-two punch/brace back through the surf to rejoin Jay, Wild Bill, Sam, and Ben who hadn't been driven to such questionable (and desperate) measures. Regrouped, we paddled a short distance to a surfless landing on Whaler's Island in the mouth of Calmus.

Curse of the Coho

We ate lunch, then I fell into a contented snooze on the pebbly beach, my ego inflated to proportions exceeding my belly, dreaming of treacherous surf landings on beaches with posted signs warning, "Rolling Forbidden." It was during this happy shuteye that the Curse of the Coho reared its silvery, gilled head.

Wild Bill is a consummate fisherman, skilled and experienced in the ways of rod and reel. The day before launching out of Tofino, he had consulted with local fisherman, bought his license, and shopped for the best lures. We were five days into our trip when we landed on Whalers Island. During those days, Wild Bill had his line in the water many times, sometimes trolling from his kayak, other times casting from shore. Though fish were clambering out of the water all around him, all he managed to catch were a few confused snags and several lengths of limp, brown seaweed.

With his gear under arm, Wild Bill was trudging toward an outcrop of barnacle-covered rock on Whalers when he met up with two young Nuu-chah-nulth lads. The kids told him they had just seen a large Coho salmon on the other side of the small island. Wild Bill hiked over to the designated spot, lured his line, and whipped it out to sea. Immediately he felt a tug, then something big ran with the line. His story blurs at this point, but after an unspecified time and a concentrated battle of wits, Wild Bill landed the big Coho. He was delighted, we were all happy, savoring the tender, pink meat in advance of the evening's meal. Wild Bill filleted the big Coho on the beach (along with two other fish caught off the same promontory) and left the remains for the bald eagles who were queuing up in nearby trees.

Back at Milties later that afternoon, we spotted another sleek creature emerging from the sea at the opposite end of the strand. Grabbing our binoculars, we dialed in for a closer look. A long-legged female, clad in a bikini, was shaking saltwater out of her hair and heading for a towel draped on the sand. Her camping gear was still loaded on the back deck of her kayak, close to the tree line. We approached and invited her to our camp for fresh salmon later that night. At the appointed time, she arrived—still wearing that splendid bikini—with a load of firewood and a bottle of spiced rum. On his first bite of fire-grilled salmon, Wild Bill started coughing and his eyes watered a torrent. "I think I've got a bone stuck in my throat," he croaked. More hacking and coughing, but the bone wouldn't free itself.

Now, I'm not one to draw hasty conclusions, but I will venture several possibilities for Wild Bill's bone-stopping ordeal. (1) Normally a moderate drinker, he tipped back too much spiced rum, dulling his senses; (2) that bikini took his breath away, which caused the bone to jam, or (3) it was the Curse of the Coho, the fish rising from the grave to haunt him. Whatever the cause, Wild Bill found himself under the surgeon's tweezers the Monday after our return, in one of those outpatient-made-for-TV episodes where he's asked if he's signed a power-of-attorney, is knocked out with a general anesthetic, and surfaces an hour later to learn there was no bone in his throat.

Reminders of San Francisco Bay

Friday morning (our last day on Clayoquot Sound), we set off for Tofino. Andrea, the bikini-clad kayaker and a field researcher studying endangered marbled murrelets, led the way. A former guide, she knew the safest and quickest line to our home port. Along the way, we stopped to gander at one of the sound's largest red cedars, dubbed the Hanging Garden Tree. Having lived in northern California with giant redwoods, it wasn't the big tree that caught my fancy, but the red cedar/Sitka Spruce boardwalk that led to it through dense forest. A confirmed Greenland paddle user, I couldn't keep my eyes off those straight-grained, light-weight planks. I've carved all my paddles from red cedar, so I was smitten by the blonde spruce. My appetite aroused by that outing, I stopped at three lumberyards the next day on our way to the Nanaimo ferry, but none of the yards had paddle-sized boards.

In Tofino, we bid farewell to Andrea over a six-pack of cold beer (ok, it was two six-packs), then Sam, Ben, and Wild Bill (eyes still watering, an unscratchable itch deep in his throat) paddled back to the motel where we had reserved rooms for the night. Meanwhile, Indiana, Jay, and I took one last jaunt, this time down the open coast south of town. While Milties conjured up images of tropical isles, this section of coastline was a dead-ringer for the Monterey/Big Sur/Carmel coastline south of San Francisco . . . waves and steep cliffs, heavy salt spray, rock gardens, shell-encrusted islets, white sand beaches.

That last paddle made leaving Clayoquot Sound a bit easier, knowing we could see more of the same close to home. Maybe it was our fame preceding us, but the toll takers at the Nanimo ferry Saturday morning didn't even bother to measure the trailer, they simply waved us through. After the crossing , we reversed the 20-hour trip that had brought us north. Our retreat was uneventful, though those of us imprisoned in the back of Indiana's SUV (definitely not designed for people with legs) discover at trip's end that the foot pegs in our boats were now set too far forward.

There you have it, the long and short of our trip to Clayoquot Sound.

Stats

Distance: Twenty-two hundred by land, 50 by water.
Speed: Seventy-five mph by car, 2 knots by kayak.
Time: Ten days in and out of the water.
Spray factor: Every so often.
Dessert: Lots.

45. Post B.C.

First paddle since B.C. and nine of us put in at Corte
Madera Creek at the stroke of six. We were, in nonalphabetical
order, Wild Bill, Zeke the Younger, Adam's Dad, Rick, Jay, Gristle,
me, Danny, and Now-'n-Again Ben. I tried alphabetizing the list,
but it didn't make our ragtag group look any better.

Gorgeous evening, but you've heard that before. Warm,
calm with a gentle westerly twinge. Feigning decisiveness, we let the
current lead us by the paddles toward Tiburon, that well-keeled
village of privileged folk. The topic of conversation was the B.C.
trip, a week past now and just a wet dream of fading delights for the
work-shirking six who braved the 49th parallel: Indiana, Jay, me,
Now-'n-Again Ben, Sam, and Wild Bill (we appear much more
formidable alphabetized).

Tales were told, questions asked Thursday evening—you
had to have been there to appreciate the ramblings. A time and a
place for everything (except rap on a classical station), B.C.'s
printed interpretation will fill the ether before the ice caps melt
(sometime soon, maybe next week).

Sun down and out before we got back, the dock at Corte
Madera Creek was fading fast. Overcome by a blast of testosterone,
Jay and Rick had sprinted back to the take-out and were
vaporwhere by the time the rest of the group pooled in. Danny,
outfitted in a brand new Eddyline Night Hawk acquired the night
before, used voice control to convince us slackers the evening was
still young and that we should paddle further up the proverbial
creek. Up and back by 10 PM on an almost moonless night, we
played hide-and-seek with the dock, but were too whipped to care.
Joe's was still open, and the evening concluded at the cactus berry
bush.

Stats

Distance: Optimal.
Speed: Slower than Jay and Rick.
Time: Maybe four hours.
Spray factor: Not tonight.
Dessert: A warm bed when I got home.

46. Churn

What started out to be a group paddle from a new launch site in the East Bay turned out to be a solo churn in our regular Marin haunts. Danny had suggested we launch from the Richmond Marina and explore the islands and park lands on his side of the bay. Six o'clock was departure time.

After 45 minutes of nudging bumpers the three miles from my house to the Richmond-San Rafael Bridge, I steered the pickup onto the paved lane escaping from San Quentin Prison, pulled out my binoculars, and gawked in awe at the eastbound lanes floundering to Richmond. It was a Morse code of flashing red taillights, the epithets they spelled out prime targets for Internet filtering software and unfit for this email. It was not a pleasant sight. It also was 6 PM.

San Quentin harbors a fine little beach, ideal for launching, but this evening the sand and water were littered in windsurfers, their sails flapping like fly wings over spilled sugar. I circled back on less traveled roads and parked in front of the concrete ramp at Bruno's in San Rafael. Little rollers were streaming into the harbor entrance, an unusual sight. Outside the channel's mouth, the water was agitated, churning for a little pickup game of one-on-one.

Definitely strange behavior, particularly for this time of year (second to last day in August). We'd paddled out of Bruno's the week before, and the bay had been apple-skin smooth, hardly a blemish. Tonight, the wind was flag-snapping rigid and blowing out of the west. A pacifist at heart, I took the path of least resistance and let the gusts blow me east.

Sprayskirted in the boat was like being strapped to a mechanical beer-hall bronco, the wind flailing the water one way and the incoming flood trying to take it somewhere else. I figured if I stayed close to shore, the tide would send me home if I got bucked off. But along the breakwater just outside Bruno's, the water was rebounding off the rocks and turning on itself, a thrashing Jekyll/Hyde, tangoing nowhere in particular. I moved further away from the confusion and 50 yards deeper into the bay.

The kayak handled well, hanging together despite being twisted five different simultaneous ways in the three-dimensional melee. But, dancing an Escheresque five-step's not all that comforting and I begin to have grave doubts. Frankly, I'd rather be in that beer hall watching someone else feed the bronco's meter.

"You're a coward is what you are," says the water, slapping my face five quick beats to the measure.

I couldn't have said it better myself and begin wondering how a coward would get himself out of this and still save face (saving face is very important). A friend of mine lives next to the water just around the spit from Bruno's. He's got a little sandy beach in front of his house I could land on. I should be neighborly and pay him a long, overdue visit. I feel better already.

Paddling into his cove buoyed my spirits even more. I'd been running in a beam sea, the waves breaking along the length of my boat. Now the waves were directly behind me, and I was surfing their faces. "Cool" I thought and glided right up to the fellow's beach with hardly a paddle stroke. Didn't look like anyone was home, though, all the blinds pulled down, no porch light. Didn't bother me, cause I was cool now, riding those waves, and I just kept on going.

The cove eventually curved round to where I was paddling in a beam sea again. From cool to coward in a whitecap. "Ok, it's time to head back," but before I can make the turn, I see three teenagers on shore, sitting on a public-works bench, caps turned backwards, a big black boom box at their feet. Looking at me, smiling, three thumbs up. I manage to get one of my thumbs up without taking my hands off the paddle. Bigger shore-side smiles, lots of white teeth now. This time they give me the clenched fist raised high in the air.

Oh jeez, THE clenched fist.

I'm still a coward, but I can't turn back now, I can't let those kids see me turn back. I keep on paddling. At the far end of the cove, I manage a glance behind and the three are still on the bench. Maybe looking my way. Probably thinking I'm all right for an old guy, hanging out in chop like this. (Ego strokes are important, almost as important as saving face). I round the cove's corner and keep heading east, past the rock quarry and on to the tip of Pt. San Pedro. My eyes are burning from the salt water and my sinuses fill up faster than they can drain.

Pt. San Pedro is good. Rarely does gnarly water dare go round the point. It's the law, and I've only seen it violated once, when The Storm of the Century ripped through last February, doing whatever it pleased wherever. This, however, is no storm and sure enough, on the other side of the point, the water morphs its tough Hyde into an orange-dimpled Shirley Temple.

"The wind'll die down once the sun sets," Shirley whispers in my ear, and I meander over to China Camp Beach to wait it out. Getting out of the boat is great, stretching is great, eating a snack is great, but best of all is letting the water drain out of my sinuses. By the time the last drop splashes into the brackish puddle at my feet, the sun is gone.

Rounding Pt. San Pedro in the opposite direction, I discover the wind is still smokin' (but maybe not as hard) and the water is still auditioning as a contortionist for the Cirque de Soleil (but maybe not as seriously), but I can't be absolutely sure because it's pretty dark, even though we're only two days shy of a full moon. But what I can't see doesn't bother me (out of sight, out of mind), and the trek back to Bruno's is blindly invigorating rather than discouraging.

It takes longer to reach home port than I had figured, and I'm toast when I pull onto the ribbed concrete launch ramp. Slouched in the boat under one of the dock's headache-bright arc lamps, my neck and shoulders throb. Watching trickles of water dribble from my nose onto the sprayskirt, a young kid rolling a garbage can from Bobby's Fo'c's'le, which has just battened down its kitchen, passes by.

"You been paddling alone out there tonight?" he gestures at the blackness to his left.

"Yeah," I nod.

"Man," he says, "you gotta be crazy."

Well put.

Stats

Distance: Six miles.
Speed: 2.2 knots.
Time: 2.75 hours.
Spray factor: Every which way.
Dessert: I wish.

47. A Perfect Twelve

Twelve. Thursday's paddle was a 12, just about the highest ranking a trek can get. If anyone's going to fully appreciate our outing, it'd be a 12-year-old kid.

Nine of us put in at Corte Madera Creek just after 6 PM: Gristle, Zeke the Younger, Sam, Albert, Indiana, Mike (a friend of Indiana's), Danny, Wild Bill, and I. Despite an ebbing tide, we opted to paddle against it up the creek. After several minor diversions, we warily circled the object of our desire at creek's end—the permanently gaping mouth of one of Marin County's longest water-filled storm drains.

Walls just far enough apart to paddle between but not turn around in made it an exceptionally special treat. If you panicked in the tight confines, it would have to be a backward paddle to freedom. Fortunately, the tunnel's utter darkness made it impossible to tell just how narrow the passage became, and we paddled on, blissfully ignorant of what we couldn't see. It was the noise that was worrisome.

The clonking of boats against concrete walls gradually reached such fretful levels, we flicked on our flashlights and headlamps. Our path brightened, we were able to steer a straighter course and the jittery noise of collision faded away. But there was something disarming about the light.

Claustrophobia has less bite when surrounded by darkness. Darkness offers unseen hope. If we bumble around in the void long enough, or so the theory goes, surely we'll stumble through the door that must be there. But once the lights blaze and we see there is no way out, claustrophobia really puts the squeeze on. It may have been that squeeze that sent several of us back-paddling to Corte Madera Creek (to be fair, our hulls were scrapping bottom just about the time we flicked on the lights, which might have accounted for the defection more so than the big squeeze).

The thin water finally petered out completely, and we beached our kayaks in a drift of mud and rock in the middle of the tunnel and set off on foot. Round one distant corner, we spied the proverbial light, but before we could get to it, another smaller tunnel split off to our right. The opening was just large enough to swallow a six-foot biped stooped at the shoulders. Do you go for the light, or do you explore the unknown?

No brainer.

In the larger storm drain, we could traipse three abreast; in this one, it was single file. Lots of soft, squishy mud in the tunnel's mouth, but that dried up the further we went. After quite a hike with a number of twists and turns, we reached the end, a place of knee-deep stagnant water that smelled like the final resting place for cats and squirrels. We waded through the sour quagmire and emerged into a neighborhood creek. Above us was a white concrete railing bordering the two-lane street we had just trekked under. We climbed up the side of the creek and were greeted with a surprisingly shrill shriek.

I suppose we did look a little unusual leaning over the rail—grimy hats, mud-covered life jackets, sprayskirts a bit on the ragged side, black wetsuits underneath—and the little girl had every right to scream when she saw us. The little kid was a real pro, too, her bellow on the same cinematic level as the scream Julia Adams belted out when the Creature pulled her down into the Black Lagoon in 1954 (now, that was a movie to remember). When the 10-12 year-old finally recovered and saw we were harmless creatures-- though she did keep a respectful distance—she asked what we were doing ("inspecting storm drains").

"Ever been down there?" we asked.

"No."

"Anybody you know ever been down there?"

"Uh uh."

We chatted a bit longer, she eventually left (no doubt having heard enough to tell her friends a good tale or two), we considered eating dinner at a nearby café but thought better of it, and then returned to the underworld. Back in the depths, I scanned the narrow surroundings remembering what the youngster had said.

Sure enough, not a scratch or smear of graffiti anywhere. Not one disgusting word or phrase, no amateur anatomical sketches, not even an impassioned love soliloquy scrawled on the wall.

No sign of neighborhood kids!

This is just the kind of place you sneak off to so you have something really good not to tell your parents. It's where you smoke your first cigarette. It's where you disappear with your best friend to discuss things you absolutely, positively don't want anyone else to hear. It's where you learn self-expression through rustic poetry and gutter art.

It's also a place where you learn to read a tide chart, 'cause you don't want to be down there when it's flooding. Without question, this is one of those rare places that's a perfect 12.

Stats

Distance: Eight miles.
Speed: Three knots by water, two by storm drain.
Time: Exciting.
Spray factor: No factor.
Dessert: My lovely wife Sandy showed up at Joe's after the paddle and, together with the rest of the crew, bought me a berry-flavored ice cream-filled treat to celebrate my b'day, the big palindrome.

48. Madness

After three days of madness, our paddle Thursday evening was more than welcome.

We met at Buck's a little before 6 PM, but instead of putting into the water immediately, we drifted over to the little wood cabin that serves as parttime tavern / hang-out (the beer cooler open until 6 PM when Will, the de facto proprietor, locks it up, and the hanging stretching into the wee hours).

Our mostly harmonious sextet (Wild Bill, Sam, Indiana, Gristle, Zeke the Younger, and I) shanghaied the last bottles of beer before the cooler closed for the night and gathered around a splintered picnic table in the trampled dust out front. We sipped the cold brew and made idle chatter with the locals. A subdued bunch we all were, physically and emotionally burned out from the week's tragic events. I, for one, have resorted to popping over-the-counters at night to sleep. I'm probably going to lose some of my hard-won ranking as a professional napper by admitting this, but it's the truth.

Conversation rarely rubbed up against what was foremost in our collective of minds. The sudden death of all those people Tuesday had sucked the spirit from us, and there's still a siren of disbelief and pain in my head that hasn't let up. I'm sure the others were hearing it, too, that prolonged wail dragging down our usual light-hearted buoyancy.

Of course, there's that other more pragmatic damper that was weighing heavy on us: what are we going to do now? From the words I've seen light up the screens of chat groups and mail lists on the Internet, from random callers on radio and TV talk shows, from the comments of friends, something has to be done. But exactly what? There the consensus ends, and the feeling of unease begins.

Already a close-to-bitter polarity of opinion has mushroomed up. My own thoughts keep creeping back to my readings on the American Civil War where public opinion --just as polarized then as it is today—ignited into a catastrophe of families, friends, and neighbors heaping incredible harm on one another. Perhaps that's why we were so subdued at Buck's, unconsciously hoping that by avoiding the issue, we wouldn't be swept up in the shadow of the mushroom.

A single beer a piece will only go so far, and after milking those last bitter sweet drops for all they were worth, we put into Gallinas Creek and headed out into San Pablo Bay. Unlike the tumultuous happenings of the week, the bay was placid, not an ounce of conflict or aggression in her soul. My own anxieties and fears dissolved in those waters in less than a dozen strokes, that's how powerful the Water Goddesses are.

Noticeably more buoyant, we paralleled the coast to China Camp Beach. The little cove is a great place to take out, the sand fine and the rocks small and rounded by time. I was paddling my wood Tern, a high-spirited boat that can't contain herself when she spots a beach, leaping as far as possible from water to shore. This evening she managed to push half her shapely hull onto the sand before friction overpowered her.

We hung on the beach till just before sunset, the gray of water seeping into sky. Indiana and I wanted to paddle further up the coast to see what the Sisters were up to, but we met passive resistance from the rest of the pod ("sure, go ahead; you can catch up with us later"). A compromise, we agreed to visit a duckblind or two on the way back to Buck's. Still in a wandering mood, Indiana and I leaned deeper into the horizonless bay in the general direction of once-seen duckblinds. The others silently voiced there disapproval by paddling toward a still-visable, closer-to-shore blind.

It was dark, this moonless night. For what seemed the longest time, Indiana and I paddled toward dark splotches against an even darker backdrop. One splotch, slightly larger than the others, seemed promising, and we headed in its direction. It turned out to be a very fast splotch, and we were only able to catch it after hectic pursuit. It was a sturdy structure, home to at least two large ducks who took to the air at our approach. Passing through three door-sized, brown-dry palm fronds hanging from a wood cross piece, we paddled into the airy innarts of the blind-turned-aviary. Well made with a large enclosed resting area (big enough for a flock of ducks), we stowed away the idea of returning one evening to join the birds for an overnight.

Navigating in the absence of light back to Buck's, our two kayaks—Indiana's glass and my wood—kept butting bows, kicking up a real spray, a difference of material opinion mushrooming up between them. We tried to let them settle those differences on their own terms, but the niggling continued. Interceding on their behalf, we kept the strong-headed boats a respectful distance apart, knowing they'd work out their grievances once the spray had a chance to settle.

The blind skirmishing at an end, the paddle to Buck's was peaceful. We regrouped on the far side of the channel across from the take out and floated in relative silence for another half hour, amazed by the constellations in a clear, planeless sky. Two shooting stars briefly lightened the heavens, which we all took for a good sign.

Stats

Distance: Further than anticipated.
Speed: Moderate.
Time: More than enough.
Spray factor: Serenely calm.
Dessert: Curling up real close to my sweetie when I got home.

49. Babes in Toyland

We could've been at the Bezerkeley Marina, catching windwaves whipped up by the westerly breezes that fetch across the bay. But we weren't; we were just off the east tip of Chard Island beyond Bruno's catching windwaves whipped up by breezes that didn't have any fetch at all, windwaves that didn't have reason to be there. That's how strange things are these days.

Those unaccounted-for windwaves surfed Gristle, Danny, and me a good-hearted nautical mile and some odd metres to the usually—this time of season—staidly stoned Sisters (Grindle and Myrtle), who this evening were behaving like two old gals hyped up on Juan Valdez' finest dark roast Colombian blend.

The tipsy waves that carried us to the old Ladies' open arms were as orderly as the high-kicking toy soldiers in that 1934 Laurel and Hardy flick, "Babes in Toyland" (aka "March of the Wooden Soldiers.") Like those cinematic dolls with their wood popguns and painted-on serious faces, row after methodical row of slate gray windwaves filled our big screen this evening. And just like those soldiers breaking rank at their first encounter with Silas Barnaby's Bogeymen in the caves under Toyland, our waves collapsed into confusion when the craggy Sisters loomed into view. Pandemonium, it was, hapless waves darting this way and that, toppling into one another, tripping over their own troughs, most pulling themselves up, but some spluttering below the surface, a splatter of white foam the only hint they'd ever been there.

As independent observers (if you can believe that bit of high-seas naivete), we were free to bumble through the chaos. "Bumble," though, may be misleading, suggesting, as it does, that we had some control in the matter. This, of course, was pure fantasy, the stuff of scripted movies and salty hubris.

Gristle and I had just eased around the south end of Grindle when a confusion of water bucked off the Grande Dame's rough hind quarters and caught up the old guy and his kayak in a swift moving retreat. The horde passed me by, and, bobbing in their wake, I watched Gristle being assimilated into their unruly ranks. Resistance, of course, was futile.

The rows of retreating waves increased in size till there was nothing to be seen of Gristle. Then a giant fist of water rose up, and clutched in it's fingers was my friend and his boat. Gristle's paddle was spinning like a prop on a plane, and he bounced down the fist's wrinkled palm just before its fingers closed tight.

The hand's foaming nails brushed the stern of his boat, but Gristle scooted out of reach and down the long slippery arm. In front of him, a steep chasm of swirling water opened up. It didn't look good, friends, no, not good at all. It was one of those Saturday matinee end-of-episode scenes where you leave the theater hoping the writers would—in the intervening week—script the hero from his plight in spectacular fashion. But it wasn't to be this night. Not spectacular, anyway. Just before the sexagenarian was about to tip his fancy for the last time into the dark waters, the skittish waves broke rank, scattering hither and yon, and Gristle and his craft coasted to a safe and lackluster halt.

If not for one startling fact, it was as if nothing out of the ordinary had happened, as if this tale were just another poorly plotted narrative destined for the midden heap of rejection slips. But something truly amazing had happened on that tumultuous ride: Gristle's hair and goatee were now a shock of pure white, a copy-cat clone of the wild white caps that had almost trampled him.

I swear on a straight-grained, knot-free, Sitka Spruce Greenland paddle that I'm not making this up. Hair as white as the surf. A goatee as shocking as a pigeon's roost. For those of you who can view JPEG image files, I've attached a photo so you can see the untouched truth for yourself.

Live long and keep your head above water.

Stats

Distance: Shocking.
Speed: Unbelievable.

Time: Miraculous.
Spray factor: Intense.
Dessert: A couple handfuls of mini chocolate chip cookies the PTSA served up at the end of open house at the local high school right after the paddle.

50. Old Farts

I've never been a great fan of skylines . . . always considered them a symptom of architectural hubris. Stubby-legged critters that we are, I reckon our brick and mortar creations as attempts to reach up and add the heavens to our sphere of influence, new spatial markets to tap, as it were.

IMHO, nothing can substitute for the silhouette of a craggy, windswept mountain peak spotted with a few spindly, oxygen-challenged pines . . . unless you happen to be paddling around Angel Island in the dark.

And paddling around Angel Island in the dark was what seven of us were doing Thursday night. If you'd had lights, you would've seen Danny, me, Wild Bill, Jay, Zeke the Younger, Gristle, and Truckee Steve circumnavigating the water-bound hillock just south of up-scale Tiburon. Without illumination, you would've spied nothing, zippo, zilch, a vacuum . . . except 360 degrees of star-bright skyline.

I'm still not a Tower-of-Babel skyline type of guy. Tonight, though, the radiant output of our architectural loftiness made an impression on me. A crystal-clear evening, the lit-up towers and high-rises that encircle the bay (San Francisco, Oakland, Marin, Vallejo, and the endless burghs in between) blistered like a ring of fire at the heaven's horizon. Suspended in black, we were looking outward from the innards of the Milky Way through a galaxy of would-be suns.

Great sights in all directions, for sure, except in our own little kayaking void. We could hear each other's paddle splashes, but visual contact was temporarily suspended, not to resume until sunrise, some hours distant. Danny suggested we each pick a number from 0 to 6 and occasionally call it out in sequence to give us substance.

"0, 1, 2, 3, 4, 5, 6." Everyone there.

"0, 1, 2, 3, 4 . . . 6. Where's Truckee Steve?"

"I'm over here. I thought you guys were headin' this way."

And so it went all the way back to Schoonmaker Cove, a most interesting and numerically complete evening.

Another interesting equation added itself to the evening's paddle—just before dark, we pulled into Quarry Beach on the east side of Angel. The sand, above the high tide line, was a jumble with kayaks. Splendid boats and fancy gear, but not a single paddler. We hung out on the beach for half an hour, munching snacks and slurping beverages, but the boats' power sources never showed. It wasn't till the following Sunday's weekly mountain bike trek over Mt. Tam that I learned from Adam's Dad who the missing paddlers were: a dozen or so Outward Bound guides were in training and camped up the hill from the beach that night. Far enough away that we couldn't hear them and they couldn't hear us.

A Sunday for solving nautical puzzles, I also learned the Bermuda Triangle is no longer fodder for "Unsolved Mysteries" or "Ripley's Believe It or Not" TV episodes. Scientists now claim to know what happened to all those ships and planes: methane hydrate.

I have it from a reliable source that smelly methane (the gaseous stuff of intestinal disorder) sinks to the ocean floor, sea creatures scatter, and, under pressure in cold water, the methane morphs into methane hydrate. The unstable chemical compound just sits there in a lump, waiting for something to stir it up. When it gets really agitated, the gas makes a break for the surface in large bubbles. Ships flounder in these lighter-than-air blobs, and sparks from airplane engines can ignite the highly flammable gas.

So, how do we make the Bermuda Triangle safe for the world? Go to the source, and keep old farts off cruise ships.

So simple.

Stats

Distance: Eight nautical miles.
Speed: Laid back.
Time: Enough.
Spray factor: Nope.

Dessert: Punjabi pumpkin pie at the Indian Take Out—or eat it there—restaurant in Sausalito (I compromised and ate the pie on the sidewalk in front of the cafe).

51. Rules

"Hey, Lucas, how're you doing?"

"Just fine."

"You sure about that?"

"Definitely."

Just goes to show that today's youth don't understand the rules of kayaking.

We were just off Pt. San Pedro paying our respects to the Sisters, who were in a twitter about something. Must've be some in-joke, because the old gals were chortling, guffawing, and belly-laughing till the tears gushed down their scraggly cheeks. Not to mention white-tipped spittle flying every which way. A regular fit of hysteria it was.

When you're tangled up with a couple old spinsters doing a number like that, you got to be careful. No telling what they might do next . . . flop you up in the air or spin you around in a waggle of unexpected merriment. You could see the worry in us older paddlers: Gristle, Jay, Wild Bill, Danny, Now-n-Again Ben, Sam, and Dave from San Francisco (his second time with us). Cautious strokes, frequent braces, back-paddling out of crazy water. Flitty eye movement (always a dead giveaway).

Lucas, though, looked rock-solid in his borrowed boat. Zeke the Younger, who had invited Lucas to Thursday's paddle, claimed that his good buddy and almost stepbrother had never been in a sit-in kayak before. A surfer, Lucas was dialed into the water and came naturally to kayaking. But that didn't excuse him for his unruly behavior this evening.

Kayaking has only one rule and this is it: don't upstage your elders.

If it had a second rule, it would be this: make your elders look much better than they really are.

To be PC, after being asked by an older paddler how he's doing, a younger paddler should always answer, "Not as good as you, Sir."

Kayaking can be a lot of fun if everyone sticks to the rules.

Speaking of fun, a bunch of us law-abiding, mature kayakers and a handful of our spouses paddled out to a remote beach in Tomales Bay Saturday night for an overnight. The Goddesses blessed us with calm waters, clear skies, and warm weather. They also kept the Great Whites confined to the mouth of the bay, which is reputedly one of the world's largest breeding grounds for the critters.

Driving out to our launch site at Nick's cove, we stopped off at the Hog Island Oyster Company for a box of the bivalves. Lugging the raspy mollusks out to our campsite almost proved beyond the capabilities of our limited storage space (we each packed more gear for this one-night camp out than we did for the six-day Clayoquot Sound expedition). My lovely wife, Sandy, however, found the needed space in her boat and personally paddled the hors d'oeuvres to the evening's campfire.

Tomales Bay rules forbid gathering any kind of wood for fires except driftwood, and our beach had been licked clean of the legal tender by previous campers. To remedy the situation, Danny, Wild Bill, Now-n-Again Ben, and I paddled down the coast in search of fuel. We towed Gristle's tandem kayak behind us, stuffing it with the odd tangle of log and stick that came our way. Piled high and battened down with Bungee cords, we hauled the Babel of wood back to Tomales Beach just in time to start the campfire.

What a fire it was, too. The wood just the right grain, density, and dryness for an intense, smokeless blaze. The poop de grâce were cow chips we found on the beach . . . tossed into the fire, they simmered into a hotbed of fine ash. As for the oysters, Wild Bill shucked up a storm despite the loss (temporary we hope) of his wife's, Bella Claudia's, grandmother's old-time shucker. Oysters, unadorned on the half shelf, are delicious, but Gristle's wife, St. Helen, fetched up a sauce of melted butter and freshly carved garlic that turned them into a gastronomic piece d' resistance.

I can't think of anything more exquisite except for the cozy tent I shared with my sweetie after dinner.

Stats

Distance: All the way.
Speed: Laid back.
Time: Repetitious.
Spray factor: Sure.
Dessert: All kinds of goodies.

52. Baptized

Baptized, christened, anointed, initiated, and he got the interior of his kayak washed out at the same time. Zeke the Younger couldn't have asked for a more bountiful close encounter of the wettest kind.

It was one of those evenings where everything is perfect . . . except the wind, which was a bit too exuberant. Normally, we don't see windwaves in the Corte Madera Creek ferry channel; there just isn't enough fetch for them to build up. This evening was an exception.

Whistling a westerly rendition of "When the Saints Come Marching In," the wind beat up the water like white meringue on a lemon chiffon pie. The sun was low in the sky—just about to set—and the peaked and cresting shadows of waves churned up from behind loomed over us with a foretaste of what was to come.

Zeke the Younger, a quick learn but at the paddle for less than two months, finally met his waterloo under a breaking wave that was not to be ignored. Fortunately, Jay, the best boat handler we have in conditions like these, was at the Younger's side in less time than it takes to crack an egg and had the kid back in his kayak before you could spit out, "Up the River Styx without a paddle."

Stirred but not shaken, we headed to San Quentin Beach for a few minutes of R&R, a dry change of clothes for the Younger, and a calming snoot of the agave plant's best elixir. The sun now an artifact of short-term memory, Gristle and his progeny headed back to the launch while the rest of us (Sam, Wild Bill, Jay, Now-n-Again Ben, Danny, and I) ducked under the Richmond-San Rafael Bridge and headed toward Chard Island.

Mountain biking in the dark, I've noticed that I have less trouble with gnarly sections than I do in daylight (out of sight, out of mind). Tonight, I had the same sensation paddling over to and then back from Chard Island. The waves were smaller on the north side of the bridge, but they were still a challenge. Only now, we couldn't see them coming at us, even with our lights aglow. To a paddler, we all felt we had to be more at one (to borrow a purple phrase from my youth) with the boats to keep them and us upright and heading in the right direction.

The very next Saturday, the upright place to be—without question—was Hearts Desire Beach where the Tomales Bay White Shark Swimmers Association's (TBWSSA'S) umpteenth annual open water swim was being held. I helped escort swimmers two years ago, and I came away at the time thinking these folks were crazy. Nothing's changed much in two years. True, I've never heard of any great whites this far down in the bay, but then all those cute seals watching the swimmers splash across the bay just happen to be the sharks' favorite hors d' oeuvres. Makes you think twice before stripping off all your clothes (which one well-turned young lass did) and jumping into the almost-60-degree water.

Crazy these swimmers may be, but they certainly do know how to party. After returning with all their limbs accounted for, the real feeding frenzy began. Cookies, brownies, chips, dips, chili, hot dogs, salads, fruits, oysters on the half shell, and the obligatory beer flowed freely. We even got shark tattoos (too cool). The activities caught the attention of the local park gendarme, who confronted the TBWSSA meet organizer with steely-eyed glares and thick rule books. The outcome? He's on the mailing list for next year's fete.

Our bodies energized by the good food and our minds challenged by the cold beer, Gristle and I once again boarded our kayaks and paddled 4 nautical miles up the coast to Tomales Beach where we had camped last Saturday. Gabbled in boats, tents, and beach towels, the beach didn't look all that inviting, so we did an about-face and headed back to Hearts Desire.

The wind was at our backs, and though the windwaves were no more than a foot or so in stature, they were quite surfable. Unlike Thursday evening when we had to paddle with abandon (not part of the regular group) to keep even with the waves, this afternoon we had to halve our strokes so that we wouldn't outrun the little gems. An instance where less is considerably more.

Four miles of effortless surfing, a warm day, free food and drink (and one naked lady)—it just doesn't get any better.

Stats

Distance: Combined, about 20 miles.
Speed: Hairy at times.
Time: Total, maybe six hours.
Dessert: I liked the home-made chocolate chips cookies, brownies, and store-bought beer the best.

53. Two Brothers

While we were gearing up to launch out of Bruno's, a small fishing boat pulled alongside the dock.

"You fellas catch anything?" we ask.

"Yeah," the tall one says and reaches deep into a cold storage chest on the boat's decke. He pulls out a salmon the size of Milwaukee. When the tail finally exits the lip of the freezer, the guy's holding the creature chest-level to keep it from dragging on the ground.

"How much you suppose it weighs?" Gristle asks, his curiosity peaked.

"Forty pounds, maybe," guesses the fisherman.

There's a rusty, old scale at the end of the concrete walkway that hugs the launch ramp, and the fellow lumbers over to it with the salmon in tow. Hefting the fish onto the pitted hook, he squints at the numbers etched into the metal. "Twenty-five" they squeak, and he says, "That can't be right" and thumps the silvery gray side of fish. First there's the sound of blistered metal rubbing up against more of the same, then a ping as the trapped spring frees itself and stretches out a good length under the fish's weight.

The pointer stops a hair short of 50 pounds.

"My dad fished in Alaska for more years than I can remember," Gristle offers, "and he never caught a salmon that big."

"Whataya gonna do with it?" Now-n-Again Ben asks.

"Smoke it," the guy says, lugging the monster to the back of his pickup.

"Probably the best way to prepare a big fish like that," says Jay. "Those big guys just aren't as tasty as the smaller ones. Smoking's the way to go," and that was the highlight of the first half of our paddle from Bruno's to Two Brothers just this side of Point Richmond.

Glassy . . . the water out of Bruno's was almost glassy with just a few cats paws scratching at the surface. The kind of water you'd paddle across with your honey to have a picnic lunch on some grassy atoll. But we (Zeke the Younger, Lucas, Gristle, Danny, Jay, Dave, Now-n-Again, Sam, and I) didn't have any sweets with us and found the water pretty boring.

About half a mile from Two Brothers, things began to pick up. Those purring little cats paws that'd been moping around us turned into some pretty nice growlers, which eventually got swept up into a rip that runs along the east side of the shipping channel fronting Pt. Richmond. The lay of the bay there encourages an occasional standing wave or two, and that's what we got, a stationary pride of standing waves to futz on.

Standing waves are cool because you get really long-lasting rides, but surfing them is akin to ambling up a down-escalator or sipping nonalcoholic beer - you go through the motions, but never get anywhere. (On a standing wave, you simply slip down the surface of the wave, which isn't much more than a raised treadmill of water.)

Our inert surfing urges sated, we turned stern to the waves and proceeded to Two Brothers, a functioning lighthouse-morphed-into-a-trendy-bed-and-breakfast. Perched atop a knob of rock less than a quarter mile off the Pt. Richmond shore, the site is a sought-after get-away, and, sure enough, a bankroll of guests lined the white picket fence overlooking the bay.

"Any rooms available for the night?" we shouted up to a well-dressed, middle-aged couple looking down at us.

"Everything's booked up," they hollered back.

"Any chance of putting out a few extra settings at the dinner table?" They laughed and said no way, but we were pretty hungry and would have gladly stayed for a meal had the offer been made. Instead, we paddled a hasty retreat to Bruno's and dinner at Bobby's Fo'c's'le.

Met an interesting fellow in the parking lot while we were loading boats prior to feasting . . . Jerry G. turned out to be a former publisher of the former "Whole Earth Catalog," a former faculty member at San Francisco State who went mano-y-mano with S.I. Hiyakawa (former president of said school and also former U.S. senator and former supporter of the Anti-Digital Dialing League), and who suffered the same tenure-terminating fate as the former novelist and activist Kay Boyle.

But Jerry's greatest claim to fame—from our famished perspective—was his current friendship with Esther, baker extraordinaire of the Fo'c's'le's incomparable keylime pies. Definitely someone to know.

Stats

Distance: Close to six miles.
Speed: Slow to middlin'.
Time: Couple hours.
Spray factor: Some.
Dessert: The best.

54. Kava Kava

The Goddesses must've been munching kava kava root Thursday evening because the bay was very subdued – almost melancholy—and glassy smooth. Had that tropical feel to it.

Those taking part in the evening's south seas holiday were Now-n-Again Ben, Dave, Gristle, Lucas, Zeke the Younger, Sam, Danny, and me. Danny, itching to scratch his growing kayak obsession, took off early and was waiting for us at the mouth of the Larkspur ferry channel. I suppose if we hadn't been so late putting in (misplaced life jackets, locked locks, and a misdirection of sculls crossing our path), he might've greeted us with something more in keeping with the evening's balmy atmosphere. But instead of "aloha," it was more to the tune of "What happened to you guys?"

About the time we eased up to Danny (I think some of the evening's celestial kava kava was weighing on our paddle strokes), the sun was doing a swan dive behind East Peak on Mt. Tam. Marin's Municipal Water District has been torching controlled burns on the mountain over the past few months, and the dark, spiraling ibex-horned clouds rising above the mountain looked like smoke from a burn.

But it wasn't. As the sun swooned deeper into its swan song, the ibex's horns twisted from smudgy brown to ochre, then to a purer red, and finally to a deep purple that went black with night fall. The whole show lasted 10 or 15 minutes, and the water's reflective surface caught the colors and jacked them up a notch or two in intensity. Paddling was out of the question, each stroke fracturing the colors into a million wrinkles. So we sat in our boats, paddles laid across decks, and floated through the performance.

When the last of the purple dissolved away, we turned on our own lights (Danny auditioning for a bit part in the next heavenly performance with a string of red-winking Christmas tree lights wrapped around his torso) and headed in the general direction of the Tiburon peninsula. Before we could make any progress, Gristle exclaimed, "Look at that diamond bracelet jangling down the grade on 101." A bracelet, indeed, but one strung together from the sparkling headlights of norththbound cars trapped in the last half of rush hour traffic. An unbroken chain that slowly morphed into red rubies as the distant vehicles inched by us.

The night was tropically perfect, but once the Goddesses spit out the root and packed up their light show, the paddle lost its verve. With the water so lackadaisical, it bordered on boring. Like floating in a dark isolation tank. So we high-sterned it back to the cars, dressed, and four of us drove over to Joe's for dinner.

The Michener theme continued at Joe's. I'd forgot to pack a change of shoes, so I dined ala native, barefoot. Ed, the barkeep, was decked out in a south seas silk shirt and mixing up Blue Hawaiians. Could have been a clip straight out of the Elvis Presley movie, "Blue Hawaii." All the scene lacked was the King himself belting out "Rock-A-Hula-Baby." But that never would've happened because the man was last seen Thursday morning in a barbershop with the Big Bopper in Prescott, Arizona, and that's a long way from Joe's.

Stats

Distance: Five miles.
Speed: Melancholy.
Time: Tropical.
Spray factor: Sluggish.
Dessert: Mud pie.

55. Back Out of Whack

Waves crashing, auditory images of swelling chords of music... no it's not a soft-focus way of describing our night at a Mendocino Inn this weekend. It's the vista and the choice faced by the Bay Area's finest. Kayaking Brood, that is.

The options seemed to narrow with each crashing set of waves. Even the intrepid (some might venture foolhardy) Animal was daunted. "We'll spend more time bailing and flailing than paddling," intoned he.

So off they went to where the Big River and the ocean embrace. And up Big River they were poised to paddle. The Animal, in a typical burst of generosity, offered to help another kayaker, unknown to the group, launch his boat into the water. Alas, the water gods were frowning. The kayaker, who moments before had been a 90 pound weakling, turned out to be denser than a rooted redwood. With a shove, the kayak ground through the sand, digging deep enough to uncover a geological layer as yet unknown in the region.

The sand groaned against the boat, but the snap that was heard wasn't the release into water....it was the Animal's back going out.

Insisting that he could still paddle, the Animal was hauled to his kayak by the now somewhat hesitant band. Gingerly, they stuffed him in, and wondered if they should just light the jaunty Arctic Tern on fire and sail it out to sea at that very moment. For, not only was the Animal wildly disabled and in pain...but his spouse, She Who Must Be Dreaded, was on her way into town. The implications of this can only be appreciated as our tale unfolds.

Kayaking proceeded for a time without fire or mishap. The cool mist and fog sifted down and around, punctuated by seals and otters, curious about the band of humans, all rafted up and imbibing copious amounts of sardines, cheese, nuts, and various spiritous libations. The operative thesis was that there exists more than one way to tame a back spasm. Libations to bolster the spirit (so to speak) of the suffering one, is a long honored tribal tradition...observed repeatedly, it has the power to render both the sufferer and the empaths at his side insensible to the pain.

Meanwhile.....

She Who Must Be Dreaded arrived in Mendocino in the mid-afternoon, supremely innocent of the horrors about to materialize. She walked around town happily, visited the bookstore, and bought delicious cookies for her darling one. How good to have a romantic getaway planned for once!

Upon walking back to the Inn, she saw that the caravan of kayakers' vehicles was appearing out of the mist. Enthusiastically, and feeling warmly disposed toward all, she waved. Erratically, the Animal's truck swerved into the driveway and disappeared. Wild Bill and Bella Claudia's van cut the unsuspecting one off from her trajectory toward her mate. Bella Claudia used a phrase like "Now and Again Ben is depositing the Animal" and SHMBD's eyes filled with pained resignation.

"What do you mean, 'depositing'. Is he hurt?"

No eye contact-"umm...noooo...."

"Is he under the influence?!"

This time, eye contact. "No...oh, definitely not."

Suspicion lay curled like a serpent ready to strike. SHMBD trotted toward their room at the Inn-60 narrow steps and three flights up a charming, picturesque water tower. At the first landing, she met Now and Again Ben (what's he doing up here?), who gave her a quick hug in greeting and then rushed down the stairs, casting fearful glances over his shoulder.

Up the stairs and onto the uppermost landing she went. Only to be greeted to the door popping open-there stood a grinning and unclothed Animal, shower running in the background. A normal post-kayak ritual...except, the Animal was definitely, well, tilted. One hip hitched higher, grin also askew. And then it hit her--INJURY!

Flashback...

SWMBD used to be a mild mannered, understanding spouse. That was before the discovery that the Animal was attracted by motion-usually involving gravity-defying incidents such as sailing through the air unintentionally.

Over time SWMBD's dewy acceptance of the consequences of physical endangerment waned:

The two simultaneous broken ankles due to a leaping demonstration for three small sons at the beach...well, she was sympathetic, thoughwary.

Then, denial: broken Animal ribs with brief unconsciousness, well hidden for almost two hours before a confession was wrung free.

The broken thumbs on each hand were met with outright anger.

The broken collar bone did not bring the anticipated next step in the cycle, depression.

Oh no, the broken collar bone brought the ultimatum: Next time you get injured, you will heal before you come home.

Would SWMBD storm out, leaving our injured hero to his own devices in the wilds of Mendocino? Would he indeed heal before he came home?? Would he remain forever tilted and naked at the top of a restored water tower room???

What do you think?

Hint: it's not the Animal writing this report.

Stats

Distance: Longer when you're doubled over in pain.
Speed: Think snails, slugs, crab-like ambulation.
Time: Better be the last.
Spray factor: Does spittle from yelling count?
Dessert: The Last Cookie.

56. True Lies

Rubbing my hip against the back of my ear is a conundrum usually beyond my reach, but since disassembling my back last weekend in Mendocino, I'm having a heck of a time keeping the dispossessed joint out of that silly-looking appendage.

Contorted and disarranged, I was grateful for my buddies lugging OTC medicines with them on Thursday's paddle. The meds were state-approved (if you buy them from a licensed dispensary), and we poured more than the recommended capful or two for adults, which we weren't, so it didn't matter. My companions were paining as much as me because they tipped back those little draughts like they were the last bit of medicine they'd ever taste. But who can blame us—we're all into natural healing, and there's nothing better than a squeeze or two from the Goddesses' agave plant to cure whatever's got you down.

Didn't have to reach far for the little plastic caps, either. Launching from Buck's after a green-bottled soporific, we (Gristle, Lucas, Danny, Danny's friend Ken, Jay, Now-n-Again Ben, and I) eased our way across the bay to Rat Island, careful not to leave scratch marks in the baby-butt-smooth water. At low tide, Rat doesn't displace much of a footprint; at high tide, it's hardly there. It was high tide when we arrived.

With boats and paddlers scrunched ajumble on Rat's weather-worn, barely-above-water outcropping, the medicines were always within an easy snoot. It's surprising how powerfully effective these homeopathic remedies are—even before the tide got a chance to gnaw at the bottom of our Neoprene(tm) booties, we were feeling no pain.

With the sun set in its ways, we left Rat in semidarkness. Now-n-Again and I paddled side-by-side, he telling me about a "men-at-sea" flick he'd just seen by the name of "Endurance." One of those movies you'll have to go to an artsy-fartsy theatre to see. Any way, without giving away the plot or the outcome of the thrilling chase scene at the end, the movie's moral was "don't sail a wood ship to the Antarctic in the winter, especially if the guy who's recruiting says you probably won't survive." Something we all should take to heart.

Now-n-Again is sometimes here and sometimes not. He claims he's an international consultant and that this work calls him away from home a lot. A lot. Last year, he claims he was in Mongolia helping the Mongolians put together a financial package to build paved roads. Gone for almost two months he was.

Well, I looked up Mongolia in the CIA World Fact Book. From what it says, the Mongolians don't need paved roads. They don't even need dirt roads. The vehicle of choice in Mongolia is the horse. The second vehicle of choice is to stay home.

Now-n-Again is on the road again, won't be back until after New Years he says. Where's he going? "South America, maybe," he answers, "Maybe Lithuania. Who knows."

Did you ever see that Schwartzenegger flick, "True Lies"? Arnold plays a covert intelligence agent whose family, friends, and neighbors think he's a mild-mannered computer salesman. Not even his wife, Jamie Lee now-there's-a-reason-to-stay-home Curtis, suspects the truth. But whenever and wherever there's trouble on the globe, Arnold goes on business trips. Quietly saves the world. Comes home. No one's the wiser.

But I've seen the movie, and you got to wonder.

Stats

Distance: Seven miles.
Speed: Under the allowable limit.
Time: Just keeps sauntering by.
Spray factor: Drowsy.
Dessert: A wedge of mud pie with a juniper-berry-anise chaser. (Congrats, btw, are in order for Gristle who now has a fistful of grandkids, his lovely daughter Kelsey having birthed a girlchild this Saturday morning.)

57. Flatland

Bone people claim that whales long ago waddled out of the water, morphed into dog-sized critters, hung out on all fours for a time, then waltzed back into the sea because of the liquid's superior perks and benies. Well, I don't know about perks and benies, but we did meet up with a wannabe whale Thursday night growling at us from a gray balcony overlooking San Quentin Beach.

We (Zeke the Younger, Gristle, Sam, and I) weren't doing much of anything, just sitting in a fine mist on a log looking at the boats we'd just drug up on the beach. The tide was ebbing, and we were watching the water slowly meander back into the bay. Like watching grass grow. Pretty tame evening. Might've been the smell of the Younger's cheese and ham sandwich that did it, but once he had the plastic wrap off, we all felt a tremble reminiscent of the Loma Prieta earthquake behind us, then the deep-throated growl. Fortunately, the creature's owner had him tethered to a thick mooring line and hand cranked the beast back inside the stilted house.

Took my breath away, that creature did. Both Gristle and the Younger looked a bit pale around the gills. But the close encounter had the greatest impact on Sam: he went Flatland on us. Lost every ounce of dimensional prejudice in his body. He became a thin veneer of his former self. No two ways about it.

"I feel kinda weird," he confessed from his boat a bit later. "I think I've lost my grasp on reality. Nothing feels right."

In the dimensionless light of dusk, looking at Sam from abeam was ok. Almost reassuring. Sam of old, the 24-hour fitness fireplug. He was still there, a presence to be reckoned with. But straight on was a different story (by Edwin Abbott?): turning his kayak slowly around to face me, his features edged into a straight line with just a hint of substance.

Not really the Invisible Man . . . more like the Thin Man. The Nick Charles of closed-deck kayaking. Stylish, sophisticated, witty . . . with a stretch of the imagination, this could be the new Sam. A movie buff, Sam's always been partial to the well-to-do detective's partner and wife, Nora (nee Myrna Loy) Charles. Could be a match made in Flatland.

The forecasters had predicted lousy weather and fast moving currents for Thursday evening. None of that. The evening was slate-gray textureless - but a far cry from lousy - and the currents seemed lifeless. Sometimes we pick up animated water crossing under the Richmond-San Rafael Bridge going north to south, but the Goddesses' puppeteers had packed up for the evening and left the water one dimension shy of any character.

We paddled back to our launch site at Bruno's, Sam sometimes with us, sometimes somewhere else. Our fear was that he would eventually slip out of Flatland's two dimensions into the slightly more revolutionary "spaceless" realm of One-Dimensional Man (a fahrenheit-451 concept popularized by H. Marcuse - and definitely not a PC destination these days).

Before Sam could dissolve away into this unthinkable place, a fishing charter crossed astern of us half a mile from the harbor. At the time, we were scooting across three-inch-deep flat water. The energy of the boat's passing in the deeper channel behind us raised up the surface into a rolling wave, and when the wave broke and lifted the stern of Sam's kayak, we heard a popping sound (like an inflated but crimped air bladder slapping into place in a boat's bow).

The shock of the three-dimensional wave had, like a high-pressure CO_2 cartridge, inflated Sam to his former self. Back to normal, he shot ahead and was waiting for us at Bruno's when we arrived some time later. Though his transmigration between dimensions had left him uncharacteristically sated, the rest of us were starved. We trooped across the dark parking lot to Bobby's Fo'c's'le for dinner where we learned that, although Myrna Loy had never eaten there, Sean Penn had (and does). Now, if there ever was a three-dimensional character . . .

Stats

Distance: Measurable only in dimensions greater than two.

Speed: Ditto.
Time: Inconsequential.
Spray factor: Sorely missed.
Dessert: Key Lime Pie.
A special get-well to Danny who, instead of venting his spleen, recently vented his knee and shin in a mt. biking fiasco. Hope you hang together after the stitches come out.

58. The Toad

Hard core . . . Thursday's paddle was hard core. It was just Gristle and me decking it out with the elements. Actually, no one else showed because we rescheduled the paddle to Wednesday evening to avoid conflicts with Thursday's traditional thanks giving and taking.

Most of Wednesday'd been misty with occasional heavy drizzles; when we put in at Corte Madera Creek, the skies had wrung themselves out to wrinkled gray. A drop of rain fell here and there, but nothing to put a sheen on your slickers. With only two of us cluttering the dock, we were able to slip into the water quickly.

About 50 yards out, Gristle started fumbling through all the pockets and hidee-holes a state-of-the-ark kayaker needs looking for his gloves. But he came up empty handed. Having removed his little finger in a self-inflicted hack attack some years back, he's become quite sensitive to cold. He jittered back to the dock and tromped over to his pickup, but to no avail. In his boat again, he eventually spied the missing mitts stuffed at the bottom of a reclusive dry bag.

All that sculumpering around warmed us up quite nicely, and we headed out the channel past the ferry terminal into San Pablo Bay. The dredger that's been WPA'ing bottom mud the last couple months was slipping into place to begin its munching ahead of us. A short-term paddling goal, when we got to the floating ten-story crane and two-bedroom-one-bath-cottage-sized dredging bucket, the weather dos-i-do'ed on us.

Whichever Goddess had been fiddling suddenly picked up the tempo: the rain kicked in hard and the surly wind chop showed its age, all white at the pate. Figuring we'd have an easier time of it, I suggested we head over to San Quentin Beach, but Gristle was high stepping for a longer paddle and led us across the near end of the bay to the Tiburon peninsula.

The wind was line dancing out of the southwest directly at us. We were both in our little Arctic Terns and took a lot of face spray. With slightly less volume in the bow than bigger boats, Terns tend to knife through rather than glide over chop taller than eighteen inches. Bow blow usually ends up on your face while water running down the foredeck adds to the scrubbing.

About 1/4 mile from land, we fell into the lee of the peninsula, the musicians broke for R&R, and all was suddenly calm. Gristle spotted the mouth of a channel we'd been down four months before, and we headed into it. Pickleweeded on both sides, the channel slunk this way and that, all the time sucking in its middle until it was just a trickle of its former self. I climbed out of my boat, stumbled across the rusty pickleweed, and hiked up a berm thinking the channel we really wanted was behind it and that we could port our boats over and continue onward. Another channel was there, but it sported more bottom mud than traversable water.

We stayed in our narrow-gauge waterway, picked up the kayaks' bows, and waltzed them around to face out. A 1/4 mile past the channel's mouth, the musicians resumed playing, though this time the tunes were more hip hop . . . the kind of sounds you'd bounce around to at a 50s sock hop. The Everly Brothers. Wayne Newton. Early Elvis.

If you're more into amusement parks than sock hops, then we were on the late, great Mr. Toad's Wild Ride at Disneyland. Circa 1955. The most hyped ride at the time was Tomorrowland's Jetson-shaped space buggies, which you piloted with stomach-churning imprecision around a tall metal pole. But it was Mr. Toad's Wild Ride in Fantasyland that garnered the longest lines. Two seats on a bumpy track, the ride carried you through Toad Hall's corridors of darkness, scratchy-voiced cardboard figures springing out of ragged crevices that made your heart skitter. Once the ride jolted to a stop, you'd run to the ticket booth, buy another go-round for 35 cents, and worm your way back into the middle of the line.

The only difference between the Toad then and the Bay now is there are no lines and you can ride all day for less than 35 cents. Some things do get better.

Stats

Distance: Six miles.
Time: Two point five hours.
Speed: Sometimes stomach-hurling, but mainly just fun.
Spray factor: Lots of that.
Dessert: Hot green tea flavored with juniper berries, anise, and caraway seeds.

Light at tunnel's end.

Photo by Jay